Arctic Ocean Issues in the 1980's

Proceedings

Law of the Sea Institute
University of Hawaii

and

Dalhousie Ocean Studies Programme
Dalhousie University
Halifax, Nova Scotia

Workshop
June 10–12, 1981
Mackinac Island, Michigan

Edited by
Douglas M. Johnston

ACKNOWLEDGEMENTS

This Workshop has been made possible by the generosity of the following contributors whose support is gratefully acknowledged:

BRITISH PETROLEUM TRADING, LTD.

ESSO IMPERIAL OIL, LTD.

PETRO CANADA EXPLORATION, INC.

SEA GRANT COLLEGE PROGRAM
NATIONAL OCEANIC AND ATMOSPHERIC ADMINISTRATION
UNITED STATES DEPARTMENT OF COMMERCE

The Law of the Sea Institute is a project (PP/R-2) sponsored in part by the University of Hawaii Sea Grant College Program under Institutional Grants No. NA79AA-D-00085 and NA81AA-D-00070 from NOAA, Office of Sea Grant, United States Department of Commerce.

Sea Grant Cooperative Report
UNIHI-SEAGRANT-CR-82-03

Publication of this proceedings is made possible in part through the support of

THE ANDREW W. MELLON FOUNDATION

Manufactured in the United States of America

This book may be ordered from:

The Law of the Sea Institute
University of Hawaii
Honolulu, HI 96822

TABLE OF CONTENTS

ARCTIC OCEAN ISSUES IN THE 1980'S

I. INTRODUCTION

Throughout the 1970's the Arctic Ocean has been the scene of increasing industrial activity, especially on the part of the petroleum industry. With significant advances in vessel and platform technology, it is becoming technically feasible to extract the rich mineral resources of the region, both from onshore and offshore reserves of enormous potentiality. More anxious than ever to reduce its dependency on foreign supplies of energy materials, the United States attaches a high priority to the development of oil and gas supplies in Alaska and the Beaufort Sea. For similar reasons, Canada is striving to reach self-sufficiency in energy before the end of the 1980's by promoting the exploration of Arctic and offshore deposits.

For both of the North American littoral states in the Arctic Ocean, the attainment of these national goals is fraught with difficulties of a wide variety: technological, ideological, strategic, economic, political, sociological, cultural and legal. These difficulties have resulted in a sharpening of difficult intergovernmental issues, especially over questions of access, transit, and environmental protection. The stresses and sensitivities now being encountered in the political arena may make it difficult for these issues to be amicably resolved through intergovernmental diplomacy in the 1980's.

Some of the bilateral issues between Canada and the United States must be seen also within a regional context. As a political arena, the Arctic region can be conceived either in polar or oceanic terms. Broadly conceived, it consists of the eight circumpolar nations -- Denmark, Greenland (semi-autonomous), Norway, Sweden, Finland, the Soviet Union, the United States, and Canada -- and arguably also Iceland as a sub-Arctic nation. Narrowly conceived, the Arctic region consists only of the six littoral or coastal states bordering the Arctic Ocean: Canada, Denmark, Greenland, Norway, the Soviet Union, and the United States. For certain purposes account might be taken of a few extra-regional states which have traditionally or recently acquired a special interest in Arctic affairs, such as the United Kingdom, Japan, and the Federal Republic of Germany. It can be contended, however, that the Arctic has not yet evolved as a region in any politically or institutionally significant sense. Some even deny that the Arctic is likely to become a region in any non-physical sense for a variety of geographical, cultural, political, and legal reasons. Yet the Arctic Ocean, however defined geographically, can be said to be comparable with other "marine regions" or "regional seas" from an ocean management perspective, even though it must still be described in terms of potentiality rather than actuality.

With a view to focusing on these basic or special policy and management issues related to the Arctic Ocean, a group of prominent specialists in Arctic or ocean affairs were invited to a three-day workshop held at Mackinac Island in June 1981. Most of the invitees were drawn from industry and the academic community, and the governmental participants took part in a strictly personal, non-representative capacity. Reflecting the special emphasis on North American issues in the Arctic Ocean, most of the invitees were Canadian and American.

The workshop was convened, then, as a forum for the non-official exchange of expert views, and it was designed specifically to address the following tasks:

(a) an overview of government policy and planning initiatives affecting the Arctic Ocean, and of the political and diplomatic sensitivities associated with the region;

(b) an exchange of views on the application of the new law of the sea to the Arctic and on the status of unresolved jurisdictional issues in the region;

(c) a stock-taking of recent scientific research in the Arctic and a discussion of the ordering of priorities for the 1980's;

(d) an assessment of emerging vessel and platform technologies designed for the waters and islands of the Arctic Ocean;

(e) an appraisal of the role of corporate initiative and of its impact on government planning and community development; and

(f) an overall evaluation of national Arctic policy requirements for the 1980's in Canada and the United States, and of the role of regional cooperation within the context of national planning.

II. STRESSES AND SENSITIVITIES

In his introductory remarks, the workshop chairman suggested that the sensitivity of Arctic Ocean issues seemed to be the most obvious point of departure. Stress and sensitivity might even be regarded as the "dominant motif" of the entire workshop, not merely the subject of the opening session. Yet the sensitivity of these matters, especially in government and industry, was perhaps the best possible reason for convening a workshop of this kind.

The Arctic, he continued, has never been an easy part of the world to know and to "deal with". The forthcoming introduction of large-scale and more or less untried technology from the shipping, petroleum and mining sectors of industry threatened to impose additional strains on the natural environment and native lifestyles of the region. In the process of assembling and importing these technologies, the corporations have had to innovate as never before, both within and across each of these sectors of industry. The scale of risks involved has forced the Arctic-interested corporations to turn both to intercorporate and corporate-governmental coalitions, involving public as well as private entities. In the process, the actors have been forced, to some extent, to overcome their normal competitive instincts. These Arctic coalitions tend to be uneasy and uncongenial to the normal policy-making practices of their members.

Although the Third U.N. Conference on the Law of the Sea (UNCLOS III) has not dealt directly with Arctic Ocean issues in any detail, it has resulted -- or very nearly resulted -- in an entirely new legal framework for the governance of the world's oceans, including the Arctic Ocean. The complexity of the Draft Convention on the Law of the Sea, it was suggested, seems to raise more questions about rule-making for the Arctic than it answers, and to that extent it aggravates rather than reduces the stresses associated with jurisdictional and other forms of legal uncertainty. Moreover, the generally accepted trend toward extended coastal state jurisdiction, within an expanding spectrum of regimes of national jurisdiction, might be expected to have strengthened the resolve of the Arctic coastal states to resist extra-regional "encroachments," especially Canada and the Soviet Union which can apparently look forward to possessing the legal as well as the physical means of regulating transit through the Northwest and Northeast Passages, respectively.

The Arctic Ocean, the chairman concluded in his introductory remarks, might now be seen from five quite distinct perspectives:

(a) as a new frontier that presents exciting prospects of resource development, of particular value for the production of energy and certain strategic metals;

(b) as a natural environment of special beauty and scientific importance, now threatened by unprecedented risks of pollution or ecological disturbance;

(c) as an emerging arena of international relationships within the limits of a natural or physical region that has not yet acquired an infrastructure of institutional arrangements like most other regions;

(d) as an area of converging zones of national jurisdiction or control belonging to the coastal states, and by that token an extension of national systems of public administration potentially capable of effecting national policies of ocean management; and

(e) as part of a unique culture consisting of widely scattered but relatively homogeneous human settlements.

The first guest speaker of the opening session, a Canadian, began by postulating the third of these four perspectives. The Arctic, he argued, should be viewed as a political region, albeit a region still in an early stage of formation. Those interested in the region consisted of the "ice-states" (i.e., the circumpolar nations) and a number of extra-regional powers with actual or potential interests in the region for resource or transit reasons. It might be premature to anticipate the development of fully regional "arrangements" (i.e. treaties or organizations) -- and such an emergence might not be desirable in certain areas of concern -- but clearly the expanding interests in the region should be served, he maintained, by an increasing range of bilateral and subregional arrangements. Even at these levels, negotiations will often be difficult and complex.

The greatest danger arises, he continued, from the inadequacy of information about offshore resources and requirements and the lack of a clear vision by the governments of how the future of the Arctic should be shaped. The region is about to be overtaken by events, and these events are happening more or less spontaneously, chiefly as a result of industrial initiatives. Little systematic thought has been given to the serious problems emerging at the interface between government and industry. There is too much dependence on _ad hoc_ adjustments, and virtually no evidence of integrated policy-making.

The same speaker illustrated the tensions of the region by reference to the Norwegian-Soviet confrontation over boundary and resource issues, and resulting differences within NATO on how best to respond to the exercise of Soviet military power in the Eastern Arctic. The NATO ice-states, he suggested, should be making a greater effort to build more cooperative elements into their Arctic relationships in order to provide a firmer political foundation for the NATO alliance in the region.

The first major commentator also referred to the increasingly sensitive symbiotic relationship between domestic and foreign policy considerations in the Arctic. By way of illustration he referred to the current sensitivity of Canadian-Danish relations, aggravated by recent Canadian industrial initiatives. In this context he referred specifically to the Arctic Pilot Project of a consortium of Canadian corporations, which envisages the extraction of natural gas in the High Arctic, the liquefaction of the gas by means of installations to be located in the High Arctic, and the transportation of this highly explosive cargo by specially designed LNG carriers southward through ice-covered waters between Baffin Island and Greenland to re-gasification plants to be located on the East coast of Canada. This Project is a source of environmental concern to the Greenlanders, and to that extent a foreign policy issue between Canada and Denmark. Moreover, the attempt by Canadian corporations to negotiate special arrangements with the Greenlanders, who now possess a high degree of "home rule", has been construed as Canadian intervention in Danish domestic affairs, and introduced new irritants into the context of native peoples' affairs in Canada as well as Denmark. The comparability of native peoples' issues in the various Arctic nations complicates the domestic process of policy-making with respect to these issues, as well as the international process of bilateral negotiations on matters that are directly, or even indirectly, related to these issues, such as the matter of transit or resource production almost anywhere in the Arctic Ocean.

The next commentator, an American, began by emphasizing the scarcity of Arctic policy expertise in the United States outside government circles. From his point of view, it was necessary for American interests in the Arctic to be evaluated within a larger context of domestic and foreign policy considerations such as the national energy policy context on the one hand and the context of U.S.-Soviet relations in general on the other. Clearly, Canada has more at stake in the Arctic than the United States, by the test of comparative importance. It was unlikely that "Arctic policy" in general, as distinct from occasional, specific, Arctic-related issues, would acquire the saliency such general considerations tend to have in Canada.

To the question of the relative importance that should be attached to Arctic-related problems in the United States, the answer could only be given in an individual situation by reference to the actual or projected economic costs and benefits involved and the weighting that could be assigned to them, at a given time, by reference to other available options similarly evaluated within an appropriate framework of national policy analysis. The importance of transit to or through Arctic waters should be viewed by the U.S. government from the perspective of alternative energy strategies, and not as an end in itself.

In this pragmatic manner, Arctic-related issues should be dealt with in much the same way as Antarctic-related issues.

The next speaker suggested that of the ice-states only the Soviet Union had a clear sense of what it wanted to do in the region. The clarity of Soviet intentions in the Arctic owed more to a carefully developed industrial policy than to an outward-looking orientation. Russian specialists in Arctic affairs rarely showed any interest in the concept of the Arctic as an international region. This national attitude no doubt had important implications for the future of regional arrangements for the management of the Arctic Ocean.

Another commentator reminded the Workshop that there had been a significant history of international cooperation in certain areas of scientific research. In some respects the Arctic basin could be compared with the Mediterranean, not only in the geographical sense as a semi-enclosed sea but also in a functional sense as a laboratory for certain kinds of scientific research that are best conducted on a broadly cooperative basis.

Another speaker, an American scientist, pointed out that national policy planning, if properly conceived, is dependent on effective research. American participation in international cooperative research required the existence of an effective national research program, but at present the polar research resources of the U.S. National Academy of Sciences are directed at the Antarctic rather than the Arctic.

Another scientist confirmed that efforts to initiate cooperation with Soviet scientists is only too frequently frustrated by interventions in the Soviet bureaucracy, even when the suggested project has little apparent strategic significance. Much tends to be made of the one lasting success in international cooperative effort in Arctic science: the Polar Bear Convention. It is not easy to predict whether this model is likely to be followed for other purposes. The only other international scientific body with Soviet participation that has outlasted the life of a specific cooperative project, is SCORE, but the recently formed, non-governmental, Comite Arctique, based in Monaco, has not yet succeeded in attracting the participation of Soviet scientists.

The next speaker expressed doubt that the difficulties of working cooperatively with the Soviet Union in Arctic matters would be resolved by adopting a more self-conscious regional approach to Arctic cooperation. The ice-states generally do not welcome any kind of cooperation that could be construed as outside interference. At least this hands-off attitude, albeit a negative one, is a link that binds the Arctic states together in a limited sense.

Another participant challenged the view expressed earlier that it might be best to have no Arctic policy in advance of a critical issue. On the contrary, he argued, most states cannot afford to let Arctic policy-making wait for some unknown crisis of the future to descend upon the Arctic governments. There are different approaches to policy-making in different political cultures, but all Arctic states should have some kind of Arctic policy in advance of events, though not necessarily a policy of the overarching kind. He suggested that even the healthiest scepticism could be carried too far, and expressed scepticism himself about the relevancy of the Antarctic analogy.

III. PROBLEMS OF ARCTIC DIPLOMACY

The first speaker on this subject, an American, emphasized that Arctic issues have an extremely low priority in U.S. government planning. The Arctic simply does not exist as a central element in U.S. domestic or foreign policy. In the foreign policy context, the Arctic is peripheral, at best, to strategic planning, and less than central even to U.S. resource diplomacy. Indeed it is difficult to identify "the problem." One is reminded of the old adage: "If it ain't broke, don't fix it." It is recognized, of course, that certain Arctic Ocean issues are of considerable importance to Canadians, and this is taken into account, though perhaps insufficiently, in the development of U.S.-Canadian relations.

He questioned the utility of regional approaches to international Arctic problems. Regional Arctic-related organizations are unlikely to emerge, and perhaps they are undesirable in any event. Even the less ambitious task of directing Arctic diplomacy to the coordination of national Arctic policies among friendly Arctic states would be difficult, because of the disparities in Arctic-related priorities. Perhaps "benign neglect" of Arctic matters was the best policy, at least from an American perspective.

As to the need for rule-making in the Arctic Ocean, the timing could hardly be worse for any U.S.-Soviet initiative. Even though the relationship between the two powers is always subject to pragmatic "fixing", it presents an unlikely basis at present for any ambitious effort at world order building. Moreover, simple solutions of the bilateral sort (e.g. "Son of NORAD") seem to be delayed too often because of U.S. insensitivities. The prospects of arms control negotiations are dim. Even UNCLOS III, which had presented a fairly secure framework for resolving certain Arctic-related issues, seems to be in serious trouble.

On the more optimistic side, there are a number of incentives in favor of rule-making in the Arctic Ocean today, he conceded. Unprecedented commercial opportunity, for example, is almost certain to lead to governmental arrangements. The companies need security for their huge investments in the region: they cannot go it alone. The Arctic environment is likely to continue to attract special conservation and pollution control concerns. And the world-wide need for peace-keeping creates another incentive for at least minimal, mutual deterrence diplomacy in the Arctic Ocean.

In response, one participant conceded that the prospect of international cooperation in the Arctic seems to recede the farther away one gets from purely scientific endeavors, but referring to the need for technological cooperation, he pointed to a very recent effort to initiate an international cooperative effort for the collection of vessel maneuver data for application to future navigation in Arctic waters.

In reply to another expression of scepticism about the utility of regional arrangements in the Arctic, an international lawyer argued that the best time to introduce cooperative institutions is before really serious problems have to be confronted, as was done successfully in the Antarctic in 1959. Another lesson to be learned from the Antarctic, he continued, is the use of a treaty to bypass difficult or sensitive legal issues. The Antarctic Treaty had proved it was possible to put really divisive issues in cold storage for over three decades. Admittedly, a treaty approach to the Arctic would introduce difficult questions about the inclusion or exclusion of extra-regional states. Very few countries are centrally involved in the Arctic.

A political scientist questioned the importance of the debate whether the Arctic was a region. Clearly, for scientists it was a <u>system</u> for exploration. For others it was a rather rudimentary kind of geo-political region, one that might be more meaningful for the smaller countries than for the large powers surrounding it. The critical question, he suggested, was whether a semi-enclosed sea like the Arctic separated the littoral states, or joined them (as in the Mediterranean and South China Seas today). In any event the prospects of Canadian-Nordic cooperation can be discussed without introducing the concept of regionalism in the Arctic.

Another political scientist was doubtful that much could be accomplished geo-strategically at the regional level, but conceded that the alternative level of bilateral negotiations may be inadequate for the treatment of certain pervasive or systemic problems, such as navigation, environmental protection, and native rights. Perhaps a mixture of cooperative support and benign neglect was what the Arctic Ocean needed.

An industrial participant referred to various kinds of diplomatic uncertainties both inside and outside the Arctic industries, all due to the fact that industry was virtually "starting from scratch" in the region. The Arctic Pilot Project had created diplomatic problems for the Canadian government as well as the participating companies because of its potential impact on Greenland's and Denmark's interests -- not to mention the EEC in the background. But it was still too early to estimate the probable scale of industrial investment in the North: if only gas was found in commercial quantities, it would be difficult to justify the high cost of extraction and transportation in Arctic conditions. Meanwhile, the chief concerns were environmental: popular fears of a major oil spill and some scientific questions about the effects of noise in the silent North. How much employment the Project might eventually bring to the Arctic communities depended, of course, on the scale of investment that finally proved to be feasible.

Diplomacy was obviously difficult as long as so many uncertainties remained unresolved. Industry, meanwhile, was developing experience in diplomacy, especially bilateral negotiations on oil spill clean-up operations, both within the industry and with governments. In the meantime, pending the resolution of so many uncertainties, he favored the continuation of *ad hoc* bilateral arrangements.

The next speaker criticized Canadian government policy in the North as "asymmetrical": that is, much more oriented in favor of resource development than anything else. He pointed to the existence of extremely generous government incentives for oil and gas explorations: high enough, at the maximum level of entitlement, to cover as much as 93% of exploration costs. Not surprisingly, industry has taken the lead under such favorable conditions of government support. As a result, Dome and Petro-Canada, the two major Canadian enterprises in the Arctic Ocean, have developed greater expertise than the federal government of Canada in certain areas of environmental research. Dome in particular, he asserted, has a clear idea of what it wants to do in the Arctic, and how to do it, but he agreed government has very little clearly thought out, integrated policy for the North, much less a systematic Action Plan for the coming decade. In the Beaufort Sea, Canada is likely to become a world leader in sophisticated offshore technology -- even if much of that technology is U.S.-designed and built. What is needed from Canadian government is a sophisticated approach to sea use planning on the North Sea model and the formulation of a carefully designed training program in advance of a comprehensive system for the regulation of shipping through the Northwest Passage.

The following speaker agreed that Canada's Arctic "frontier policy" is in serious disarray, despite the fact that Canadian industry is on the threshold of massive developments involving unprecedented risks of several kinds. "Southern development thinking," he asserted, still dominates the approach to questions of Northern development, and this is clearly reflected in the National Energy Program. This introduces special stresses and constraints that do not necessarily reflect the aspirations of the native people. As industrial development proceeds rapidly, there is no matching progress in local political development.

Another Canadian speaker began by describing the Arctic Ocean as a region-in-the-making for certain functional purposes. In region-formation in the years ahead much will depend, he said, on the pattern of information-sharing that can be developed through cooperative arrangements. At present data-sharing is confined mostly to certain sectors of scientific research, but it is surprisingly irregular and infrequent between the Canadian and U.S. armed forces, even within NORAD, and almost non-existent among commercial entities, except when common access to research findings is required by the terms of an industrial consortium. Access to environmental information seemed especially critical in view of the scale of impending industial development in the Arctic Ocean. (By one projection, there may be as many as 1,000 vessels a year -- three per day -- traversing Lancaster Sound by the end of the century.) This comment led to a general discussion, which reflected a consensus that all the major Arctic players, both corporate and governmental, preferred the flexibility inherent in dynamic _ad hoc_ arrangements.

Another commentator took issue with the concept of a U.S. Arctic policy of "benign neglect", which he described as a "myth". He identified three levels of approach to foreign policy issues in the Arctic: the global, general (international law) level; the national (unilateral action) level; and the regional arrangements level. Almost all Arctic-related events in recent years fell into one or the other of the first two categories. If the Arctic states decline to enter into regional cooperative arrangements, they should not be surprised to find themselves facing mounting pressure for cooperative action from outside, at the global level, especially in a context of legitimate global concern such as that of nature conservation or weather control.

When the discussion turned specifically to the role of the Arctic in Canadian-U.S. relations, the principal speaker on this subject, a Canadian, began by referring to the enormous symbolic importance of the Arctic in the Canadian psyche. The American people, and even the American government, seem almost completely unaware of this feature of Canadian society, or perhaps simply indifferent to it. As a result, even the best-intentioned U.S. initiatives in the Arctic sometimes succeed in irritating the Americans' best friends in Canada, provoking a clamor that the most pro-Canadian Americans are inclined to regard as an overreaction. If the Arctic is simply not on the U.S. national agenda, as an earlier speaker suggested, then that is part of the problem in U.S.-Canadian relations. The

Arctic region may not be crisis-prone, but it has certainly generated a good deal of friction in Canadian-U.S. relations. The brouhaha over the Manhattan voyage in 1969 is a well-remembered case in point.

One is bound to recall, he continued, the fundamental differences between the two countries in the mode or style of approach to foreign policy. Recently the American approach has been characterized by the effects that flow from the co-existence of a strong Congress and a weak Executive, whereas the Canadian approach is still the result of a traditionally weak Parliament and a traditionally strong Executive. As the recent East Coast Fisheries fiasco has demonstrated, the most carefully negotiated arrangements between the two Executives can be subverted (constitutionally) by Congress, sometimes for reasons not entirely germane to the merits of the arrangement.

In other ways, Canada and the United States seem to be going in opposite directions. Canada is maintaining, if not increasing, certain government expenditures at a time when the United States is engaged in a conspicuous effort to lower drastically the level of almost all public expenditures. This, of course, is especially pertinent to the prospects of public funding of scientific research. The United States is examining the case for the deregulation of industry, while the Canadian government is increasingly committed to a policy of massive intervention in the market place, especially in high-risk Arctic-related sectors of industry. At UNCLOS III, especially in its earlier years, Canada and the United States have often been at loggerheads over important issues, and indeed they still differ markedly over unresolved deep ocean mining issues. Although many of these issues are global or at least multilateral in scope, they tend to strain the entire relationship between the two neighboring countries.

Special reference might be made to the different perceptions of the Soviet threat. Canada and the United States cooperate in the monitoring of Soviet military movements in the Arctic, but the significance of these activities is differently interpreted in the two capitals, and the Canadian authorities rarely get access to the raw data obtained. This access problem makes it difficult for Canadian defense specialists to match their U.S. counterparts in strategic analysis in the Arctic sector. In short, the present period does not seem propititious for dramatic improvements in Canadian-U.S. relations in Arctic matters.

IV. THE IMPACT OF UNCLOS III

The opening speaker at this session, a Canadian international lawyer, began by emphasizing that the forthcoming Convention on the Law of the Sea, now in the final stages of negotiation at UNCLOS III, was intended to govern all oceans, including the Arctic Ocean. The fact that the Arctic rarely received specific mention -- by virtue of an unspoken "gentleman's agreement" among Arctic and non-Arctic nations -- took little away from the general applicability of the Convention to the Arctic. The forthcoming Convention was designed to regulate ocean activities around the world, in the same way as the four Geneva Conventions emanating from UNCLOS I in 1958.

Yet in two respects it might be said that UNCLOS III had a special significance for the Arctic. First and foremost, the Convention contained a provision, drafted by the Canadian delegation, which was designed to grant exceptional powers to the coastal state in ice-covered waters:

> Article 234: Ice-covered Areas
>
> Coastal States have the right to adopt and enforce non-discriminatory laws and regulations for the prevention, reduction and control of marine pollution from vessels in ice-covered areas within the limits of the exclusive economic zone, where particularly severe climatic conditions and the presence of ice covering such areas for most of the year create obstructions or exceptional hazards to navigation, and pollution of the marine environment could cause major harm to or irreversible disturbance of the ecological balance. Such laws and regulations shall have due regard to navigation and the protection and preservation of the marine environment based on the best available scientific evidence.

It should be noted especially that this provision authorizes the coastal state, in ice-covered areas within its exclusive economic zone, not only to adopt but also to enforce its own national "laws and regulations for the prevention, reduction and control of marine pollution from vessels." This is an important exception to the general policy of UNCLOS III to preserve the self-policing powers of flag states in the context of ship-generated pollution. The original version of Article 234 was limited to a special grant of prescriptive authority to the coastal state with ice-covered waters within its economic zone, but since 1976 the addition of enforcement powers has survived the dynamics of trade-off diplomacy at UNCLOS III.

The definition of "ice-covered areas" in Article 234 is not entirely precise, but although it might be applied less restrictively, from a geographical point of view, it should be noted that the (Canadian) draftsman had Arctic waters specifically in mind.

The same speaker went further to advance the opinion that the ice-covered exception of special coastal state authority, articulated in Article 234, was already established in general (i.e. customary) international law. Even if the present Draft Convention on the Law of the Sea failed to be widely ratified, and thus did not enter into the general treaty law of nations, the principle of Article 234 would still survive, he argued, as a norm of international law. He based this view on the fact that the "ice-covered exception" -- as it is called in law of the sea circles -- has received wide acceptance among UNCLOS III delegations to the point of general consensus or acquiescence. The United States delegation, specifically, decided on a policy of non-objection, if not active support, with respect to the ice-covered exception, and this, he argued, made it difficult for the United States to deny the validity of the rule of Article 234 in the event of a last-minute treaty failure at UNCLOS III.

The other UNCLOS III provision of special significance to the Arctic was Article 123, which deals with semi-enclosed seas.

> Article 123: Cooperation of States bordering enclosed or semi-enclosed seas
>
> States bordering enclosed or semi-enclosed seas should cooperate with each other in the exercise of their rights and duties under this Convention. To this end they shall endeavour, directly or through an appropriate regional organization:
>
> (a) To coordinate the management, conservation, exploration and exploitation of the living resources of the sea;
>
> (b) To coordinate the implementation of their rights and duties with respect to the protection and preservation of the marine environment;
>
> (c) To coordinate their scientific research policies and undertake where appropriate joint programmes of scientific research in the area;
>
> (d) To invite, as appropriate, other interested States or international organizations to cooperate with them in furtherance of the provisions of this article.

Unlike Article 234, Article 123 does not constitute a special exception to a general norm, but it is clearly applicable to the Arctic basin, if the latter is conceded to be a semi-enclosed sea. The speaker argued that the Arctic does have the necessary geographical attributes to qualify for inclusion under Article 123, and asserted that in no sense should this determination be regarded as dependent on whether or not the sea in question qualifies as a region in a political sense. He pointed out that bordering states "should", not "shall", cooperate, which makes the duty less than mandatory, but that the provision goes on to stipulate that they "shall endeavor" to carry out a range of designated tasks of coordination and cooperation. Seen in the round, the Article might be regarded, like so many other provisions of the Draft Convention, as "quasi-obligatory". So qualified, the obligation applies not only to protection and preservation of the marine environment (like Article 234), but also the management, conservation, exploration and exploitation of living resources and to the conduct of scientific research. The obligation, it should be noted, is not confined to high seas areas of such seas: by implication, it extends also to areas within national jurisdiction, at least to economic zone areas beyond 12-mile territorial limits.

The speaker went on to assert that existing historic rights were preserved under the new Draft Convention, by virtue of Articles 7 and 10 and the other territorial sea provisions which had been incorporated, virtually without change, from the 1958 Geneva Convention on the Territorial Sea and Contiguous Zone. He suggested that a case could be made -- though not without difficulty -- that Canada had acquired sovereignty by virtue of historic rights to the waters of the Canadian Arctic Archipelago and of the Northwest Passage under the regime of internal waters. In conceding that the argument could be made both for and against that proposition, he referred to a recent 3-volume study commissioned by the Canadian Department of Indian and Northern Affairs which presented "impressive evidence" that the local Inuit nation had made constant use for centuries of these waters, especially in the Eastern half of the Northwest Passage, including Lancaster Sound and Barrow Strait as far as Resolute and a little further west. He noted that if the Canadian government were to grant recognition domestically to Inuit land and offshore claims based on their historic (hunting) practices, the recognition might be held out as having some international as well as domestic legal significance, strengthening a Canadian claim to sovereignty to these waters under the international legal regime of internal waters by virtue of historic rights.

The following speaker, an American international lawyer, began by observing that the Draft Convention still consists essentially of new or emerging law, which cannot be expected to resolve the entire spectrum of jurisdictional issues in the Arctic Ocean. Much of the language might be regarded as expressive of carefully negotiated legal policies or strategies, and some of this language may be of questionable validity under general international law, if the world community should fail to adopt the entire complicated "package" of trade-offs and compromises inherent in the Draft Convention. It was difficult, he said, to assert dogmatically which portions of the text would survive intact in such a contingency.

He proceeded to make a number of specific observations about the impact of UNCLOS III on jurisdictional issues in the Arctic. First, he questioned whether the sector theory could be regarded as valid in the wake of UNCLOS III. Various modes of extending coastal state jurisdiction had been carefully worked out within the Conference, but none of these modes seemed to give any further credence to the sector principle. Indeed he had difficulty in finding any textual evidence to support the view that UNCLOS III had accorded any special preferential status to the Canadian Archipelago.

Second, a good deal of ambiguity -- much of it intentional ambiguity -- had been injected into the provisions concerning rights of passage or transit under the various regimes of national jurisdiction. The Conference had endorsed the general principle that the right of navigation should not be impaired unreasonably by the unilateral action of the coastal state, and that there was an international interest in the regulation of navigation at large. Coastal prerogatives had also been conceded, but it was intended that a balance should be constantly preserved between inclusive and exclusive authority. In difficult situations, the appropriate balance might have to be sought at a more specific level of rule-making.

Third, he expressed some reservation on the question whether the Arctic Ocean as a whole qualified geographically as a semi-enclosed sea under Article 123. Although he did not wish to quarrel with the principle of cooperation expressed in that provision, it might be doubted whether the Arctic passed the geographical test, particularly in view of the open waters to the east of Greenland.

Fourth, he saw very little evidence of support at UNCLOS III for the notion of historic rights, except the reference to historic bays in Article 10(6).

Finally, he addressed himself to the question of the Arctic-related effects of a general failure to adopt or ratify the forthcoming Convention on the Law of the Sea. Even in such an event, he believed that state practice would be profoundly influenced by the general principles, ("strands of policy") woven into the text. Even if the Convention survived merely as a framework of legal policies, the "rules of the game" would be altered permanently in many areas of the law of the sea, especially in the context of resource rights. But if the Conference "package" finally fell apart, it would not be entirely evident that the world community had granted special treatment to the Arctic. The "Arctic exception" reflected in Arcticle 234 might still be conceded on an _ad hoc_ basis, but coastal regulatory powers with respect to transit would be difficult to disentangle from the negotiated package as a matter of independent entitlement. Indeed, even the 12-mile territorial sea might not be acceptable to the United States, if UNCLOS III finally failed, since it was perceived by that country as a central trade-off concession inseparable from the web of interconnected issues which made up much of the text of the Convention.

In referring to the theory of incorporation of norms into general international law, the next speaker compared the various points in time at which principles or rules contained in the Draft Convention on the Law of the Sea could be considered as becoming part of the general (or customary) international law of the sea. He referred to the chronological continuum, within which one looks for the consensual foundation of such incorporation. This continuum, he said, might be regarded as stretching, at the earliest, from the point in the past when the delegations at UNCLOS III reached an "understanding" to accept a particular norm (and "consensus" within the conference was thereby discerned) to the point in the future, at the latest, when virtually all nations have finally accepted the Convention though ratification or accession. The last point in time was certainly much too late, and most international lawyers might be reluctant to grant so much juridical significance to the establishment of diplomatic consensus or "understandings" at the earliest point on the chronological continuum. There was a lot of room for differing views on where to locate the "critical date" between these two extremes. The present juridical impact of UNCLOS III -- particularly of Article 234 of the Draft Convention -- on the Arctic Ocean depends, he suggested, on how one approaches this basic theoretical question of incorporation.

The same speaker raised the question whether there was any high seas area left in the Arctic Ocean. To this question, there seemed to be three possible answers. First, it might be contended that the Arctic Ocean, by and large, has always come under the traditional regime of the high seas in customary international law, and that the effect of UNCLOS III has simply been to extend the seaward limits of national jurisdiction. By this line of argument, it would be concluded that the high seas area of the Arctic Ocean has simply shrunken, but is to be found in the middle of the Ocean, otherwise unimpaired, in the absence of any textual evidence to suggest the contrary. Second, it could be maintained that the existence of a maritime "enclave" of high seas in the middle of a semi-enclosed sea such as the Arctic Ocean is an anomaly which cannot be supported under the new law of the sea. The littoral states of the South China Sea had taken the view that the existence of a similar "enclave" of high seas in the middle of "their" marine region was inconsistent with the spirit and intention of UNCLOS III, particularly as applied to semi-enclosed seas, and difficult to reconcile with the geographical realities relevant to questions of access. By this reasoning, the "enclave" should be swallowed up by one or more of the adjacent claimant states under the principle of extended coastal state jurisdiction. Third, it was possible to advance the view that the Arctic Ocean had never acquired the status of high seas prior to UNCLOS III, and that in the absence of any express provision dealing with the matter the status of the Arctic Ocean beyond limits of national jurisdiction remained indeterminate. This argument rested on the proposition that the Arctic Ocean was and remains *sui generis* in the law of the sea, and that an unresolved jurisdictional issue such as this requires specific *ad hoc* treatment at the global or regional level and cannot be resolved by analogical reasoning from general principles that are not necessarily applicable.

With respect to the scope of the "ice-covered exception" of Article 234, which grants special environmental rights to the coastal state, the same speaker suggested that, whether or not the Convention or the Law of the Sea is in force at a given point of time in the future, the question of the scope of the coastal state's environmental rights in the Arctic Ocean should be approached from the perspective of state *responsibility*. In choosing where, precisely, to strike the balance between these environmental rights of the Arctic coastal states and the navigation rights of transit states, the matter should be governed, first and foremost, by the recognition that these rights of the coastal state should be commensurate with the latter's special responsibility for the protection of the marine environment in ice-covered waters. Any other, purely legalistic, approach to the "balancing of rights" question in the Arctic would be a disservice, he suggested, to the need for effective conservation of the Arctic marine environment.

Several participants commented on the impact of Article 76 ("definition of the continental shelf") on the Arctic Ocean. It was generally agreed that most of the sea-bed of the Arctic would be included under national jurisdiction by virtue of the formula in Article 76, especially in the Norwegian Sea and adjacent areas. The Soviet Union, Canada, and Norway obviously were the biggest gainers of shelf areas in the Arctic as a result of UNCLOS III. The stakes were getting higher, as additional petroleum reserves were discovered in the region, putting an additional strain on countries involved in shelf delimitation issues. Reference was made to current bilateral negotiations and arbitration efforts affecting Norway, Iceland, Denmark, Greenland, Canada, and the United States.

Most, but not all, of the legal participants seemed to agree that the Arctic Ocean -- or at least a substantial portion of it -- qualified as a semi-enclosed sea in the legal as well as the geographical sense, and that Article 123 was therefore applicable to it. No one present seemed to know whether the delegations of the Arctic states at UNCLOS III had arrived at any private "understandings" among themselves about the special nature of the Arctic Ocean, its qualifications as a semi-enclosed sea, the applicability of archipelagic or sector theory, or other matters related to the extent of coastal state jurisdiction in the region. Several expressed concern that the aggrandizement of national jurisdiction in the region, to the fullest extent permitted by the provisions at UNCLOS III, would seriously imperil the future of Arctic scientific research, making access almost impossible without the permission of the nearest adjacent state.

V. UNRESOLVED JURISDICTIONAL ISSUES

This session opened with a brief presentation on the November 1980 Soviet decree clarifying the boundaries of time zones and introducing daylight saving time. Since 1930, time has been calculated in the USSR at one hour ahead of the international time zones. This is called "decree time", and the 1980 decree further introduced daylight saving time from 1 April to 1 October each year in addition to decree time, so that for six months of the year time would be calculated two hours in advance of GMT, in the respective time zones. The Decree was highly explicit for the Soviet Arctic areas as to precisely where the zone boundaries were located and thus serves as the first general indication in more than half a century of Soviet territorial jurisdiction in the Arctic. The precise boundaries would repay study for insight into the straight baseline principle, but it was evident that the Decree did not assert any sectoral jurisdiction in the Arctic. The question nonetheless remained whether the legislation could be referred to subsequently, if it were necessary to make legal use of various modes of legislative action and the doctrine of acquiescence in order to support a more direct claim to coastal state jurisdiction in the region.

[_Editor_: The 1980 Decree has been translated in W.E. Butler (ed.), _Collected Legislation of the USSR and Constituent Union Republics_ (1979-)]

The first principal speaker of this session, an American, identified what he considered to be the major unresolved jurisdictional issues in the Arctic Ocean. First, he referred to three boundary delimitation issues:

(1) the Canadian-U.S. boundary dispute in the Beaufort Sea, which was of some concern to the United States because of the exploratory activity of Dome Petroleum in the disputed area;

(2) the Norwegian-Soviet boundary dispute in the Spitzbergen area, which had already been referred

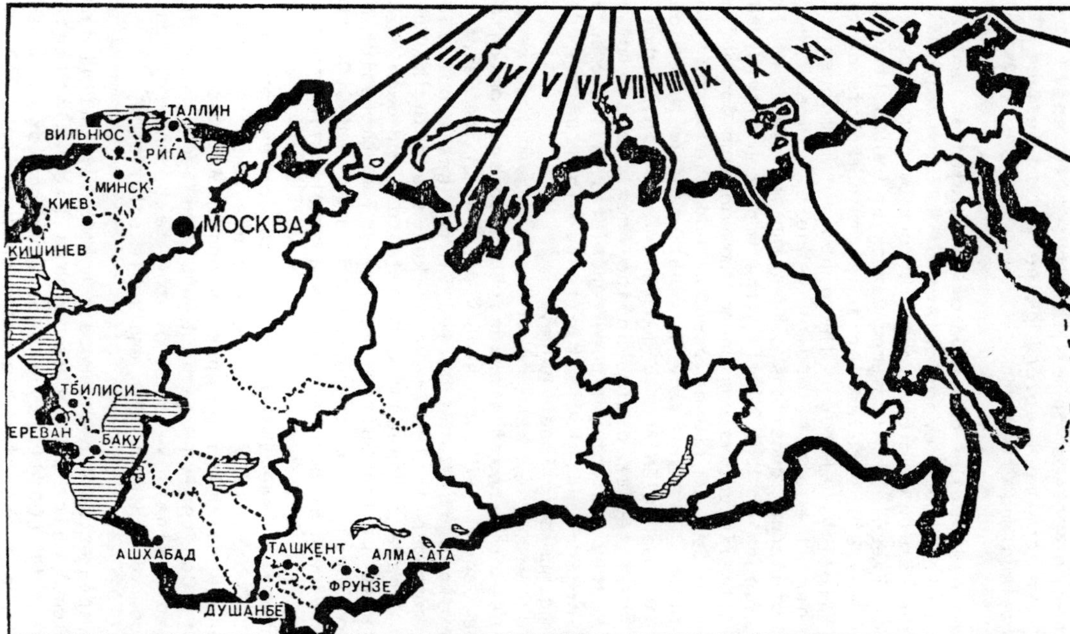

TIME ZONES IN THE USSR UNDER 1980 LEGISLATION

to as having a considerable strategic value for both parties and for NATO; and

(3) the Canadian-Danish/Greenland dispute over the northern extension of the existing shelf delimitation agreement covering the waters between Ellesmere Island and Greenland.

Second, he referred to the question of the status of Canada's Arctic Waters Pollution Prevention Act of 1970, seen now in the light of the result of global negotiations over the coastal state's prerogatives in ice-covered waters at UNCLOS III. He believed there was still objection to certain aspects of the Canadian legislation, although there had not yet been any prosecution under it against foreign vessels. Third, there was a complex of larger questions concerning the status of the Northwest Passage after UNCLOS III, the applicability of the international straits provisions under the emerging Convention on the Law of the Sea (Articles 34-45), and the validity of archipelagic theory in customary international law that might be applied to the Canadian Arctic geography. Fourth, although he considered that sector claims in the Arctic could not be taken seriously, they had not yet been repudiated by the coastal states of the region and, to that extent, might be regarded as an outstanding jurisdictional issue.

In response, the next speaker, a Canadian, commented briefly on the Canadian-U.S. boundary dispute in the Beaufort Sea. He explained that the United States has adopted an equidistance approach to the issue (like Canada in the Gulf of Maine) and Canada a "special circumstances" approach (like the United States in the Gulf of Maine). The inclusion of references to "equitable principles" in the UNCLOS III provisions was viewed by both parties as a complicating factor.

[Editor: Since the Geneva session of the Conference ending in August 1981, completely new language has been introduced into the boundary delimitation provisions in Articles 74 and 83 of the Draft Convention on the Law of the Sea. Under the new (and probably final) version of the text, the reference is to the purpose of achieving "an equitable solution".]

The same speaker defended Canada's Arctic Waters Pollution Prevention Act, which he believed had been vindicated retroactively at UNCLOS III by the achievement of consensus on the "ice-covered exception" granted under Article 234. He took the view that the Northwest Passage did not qualify as an international strait, either under Part III of the Draft Convention or otherwise. In referring to the late Judge Baxter's distinction between waterways that were actually used, and those that were merely usable, for international navigation, he observed that the crossings of the Passage had been few in number, and all had been experimental in nature. Finally, he agreed with the previous speaker that the sector theory had no juridical validity.

Most of the general discussion that followed focused on legal questions related to the Northwest Passage. Several participants stressed the importance of the Passage issue in view of the opening up of this waterway that can be expected in the late 1980's. One commentator felt it was desirable to "institutionalize, not legalize" the issue. Another political scientist agreed, stressing that "political, not pragmatic" approaches would have to be taken to the issue, in view of the symbolic importance of the Passage in the "psyche of the Canadian people".

One of the international lawyers participating explained that if the Passage was deemed to belong to the "regime of straits used for international navigation", as formulated at UNCLOS III, it would become subject to the newly defined "right of transit passage": that is, "the exercise... of the freedom of navigation and overflight solely for the purpose of continuous and expeditious transit of the strait between one area of the high seas or an exclusive economic zone and another area of the high seas or an exclusive economic zone" (Article 38(2)). This right was almost, but not quite, the equivalent of the freedom of navigation in the high seas. This would mean, he argued, that a foreign submarine would be entitled to remain submerged in transiting the Passage, since submersion was a submarine's "normal mode" of continuous and expeditious transit", as envisaged in Article 39(1)(c). In response, it was observed that the Passage issue aroused strong feelings only in Canada, but that it was neither in the American nor in the Soviet interest to try to force transit though the Passage against Canada's will.

An American political scientist argued that the Northwest Passage was not a serious issue in Canadian-U.S. relations. It should be possible, he asserted, for the two governments to arrive quietly at "accommodations", which would be acceptable to Canada as the guardian of these waters without being prejudicial to the United States' publicly declared espousal of the general principle of "transit passage", which was of enormous importance to the United States elsewhere. Canadian consent to such an arrangement might be more difficult to achieve than U.S. consent. The <u>Manhattan</u> incident had demonstrated the emotional volatility of the Passage issue in Canada: on this issue, he suggested, "the Canadian Cabinet had been captured by the rank-and-file of the Liberal Party." The inflexibility of the Canadian delegation's position on Arctic transit at UNCLOS III had been forced upon it by the explosive attitude back home. In actuality, he said, Canada's most important interests in the Arctic Ocean were developmental, but its national policy -- and legal strategy -- had been deflected to pollution control concerns. The problem, he concluded, was not one of principle, but one of reconciling two very different sets of domestic political interests inside Canada, and the problem of reconciliation presented extreme difficulties within the Canadian political system.

One of the Canadians participating in this discussion pointed to what he perceived to be a "paradox" in the Canadian position on the Northwest Passage. On the one hand, he said, environmental protection was the ostensible purpose of the Arctic Waters Pollution Prevention Act, and yet it was Canada's policy, on the other hand, not to prohibit the "innocent passage" of foreign vessels through these waters, including foreign oil tankers. Permission for such transit was apparently to be granted, without strict regulatory controls, and yet Canadian Arctic-based mining projects that were "much less environmentally threatening" were required under Canadian law to conform with environmental impact assessment procedures that could cause delays of several years, while environmental improvements were designed into the projects under review.

An American participant agreed with an earlier speaker that it might be diplomatically feasible for the United States and Canada to negotiate a bilateral treaty that spelled out specific conditions of transit through the Passage for commercial vessels. But he noted that such an agreement, however satisfactory to the contracting parties, would not be binding on third parties. Another participant predicted that Japanese commercial shipping will follow Americans into the Arctic, once successful transit through the Beaufort Sea has been effected.

One speaker suggested that the Canadian government should impose a limitation on the number of vessels allowed to go through the Passage for reasons of environmental prudence. It was a matter of degree. Some vessels were more threatening than others: as noted before, an LNG carrier presented less pollution risk than a supertanker. Some kind of quota arrangements might have to be applied to various categories of vessels to reduce such risks. Another Canadian confirmed that only environmental controls were in contemplation: there was never any intention of prohibiting foreign vessels, as such. Vessels would only be prohibited if they failed to comply with various prescribed standards of construction, design, equipment, and navigational capabilities.

At this stage of the discussion, it was emphasized by several speakers that Canada, as the guardian of the Northwest Passage, had a responsibility to invest substantially in the improvement of its shore-based vessel traffic management capabilities. Canada should "put its money where its mouth was". One should pay for "the pride of sovereignty". But one speaker raised the question whether government or industry would have to pay the costs of Arctic ocean management. Arguably, the Canadian government should not get too far ahead of what was commercially feasible: for example, in the subsidization of development of ice-breaking capability. Another limitation on the scope of Canadian public investment in ocean management, in the Arctic or elsewhere, was the degree of saleability of such an investment program within the Canadian political system. It was always politically tempting, in any country, to "have your cake and eat it too": that is, to enjoy pride of sovereignty, but not to pay for the costs of responsible management.

VI. RECENT SCIENTIFIC RESEARCH

This session began with a brief review by the panel chairman of some of the persistent problems of Arctic scientific research: the inherent difficulty of conducting year-round research in the distant North; the problem of initiating international cooperative efforts in certain sectors of Arctic science; that of mounting and sustaining long-term research; the perennial burden of underfunding (for example, the lack of a research ice-breaker in Canada); and the constraints associated with a high degree of dependency on government initiative.

The first principal speaker referred to the early history of "small science" in Arctic investigation, when most research was carried out by an individual scientist with modest funds and facilities. This was contrasted with the present stage of Arctic science, characterized by large-scale, technically sophisticated, computer-assisted, multi-disciplinary research, which requires careful design and coordination. Much of the recent research in the Beaufort Sea, for example, has been done by scientific teams focusing together on the ecosystem of the region, which can thus be subjected to scrutiny from various perspectives by different kinds of specialists within a pre-arranged framework of cost-shared investigations.

Arctic biological research has until recently been limited in its potentiality by the belief that the Arctic Ocean is a region of relatively low productivity. But the latest research shows that there is no uniform biological system in the Arctic Ocean, but rather several distinct systems of varying degrees of productivity. The Arctic Ocean proper -- that is, the Arctic basin of ice-covered waters, whose upper layers lack any demonstrable admixture of Atlantic or Pacific waters -- is perhaps the least productive marine region in the world; but the peripheral mixed-water areas of the sub-Arctic seas and bays are extremely variable, and some of these areas (e.g. around Iceland and off Southwest Greenland) are among the most productive. Reference was made to important recent discoveries explaining the surprisingly high level of productivity of certain species on the Bering Sea shelf under PROBES, a multi-disciplinary, multi-ship project of the kind that is becoming increasingly important in order to carry out modern research in the Arctic. These findings would not have been possible but for the combination of physicists, chemists, and biologists on board. This newly developed technique of collaborative inquiry represents the future approach to Antarctic as well as Arctic research, and it must be encouraged through proper long-term planning.

Until recent years research and defense were the main reasons for venturing into the High Arctic. Now the picture of scientific research is changing radically under the impact of resource development requirements. New areas of investigation are being opened up by virtue of the actual or projected impact of industrial technology: shore erosion, pollution, ice hazards, and so on. Even the traditional, basic oceanographic questions -- such as those related to ocean water movements, climatic change, and the causes and efforts of upwelling at the ice-margin -- are now seen to have a greater urgency than ever.

Meanwhile, many areas of polar research remain in a state of infancy: for example, migratory patterns of certain marine species and meso-scale structure analysis. The inadequacy of logistical support is a special problem for most areas of Arctic research. Without a serious commitment to research in this unusually difficult environment, many questions will remain unanswered. Fortunately, the general picture seems to be improving: the Bedford Institute of Oceanography, for instance, is now putting much of its effort into Northern Oceanographic research.

The next principal speaker opened by admitting that he is less concerned about the "purity of science" than some other scientists, since he can usually spread his time over a fairly large number of co-existing projects of varying kinds. Research generally can, and should, serve two or more purposes at the same time. Much more serious is the problem of attracting and keeping the appropriate scientific talent, and even more so of securing the appropriate level of technical support even for the world's best Arctic scientists. Contracting out to the universities is only a partial remedy, under the present funding system. In Canada, most of the important Arctic work is given to government laboratories. On the whole, he suggested, this system tends to result in high quality research, albeit with less money and less brilliant staff than would be assigned to the same work in the United States.

Funds are certainly scarce -- especially in relation to expanding requirements -- and competition for these funds is getting more severe each year. But public expenditures cannot be expected to rise rapidly. One looks to industrial funding as the major new source of Arctic research. Fortunately, there are, it was suggested, realistic prospects in Canada that the scale of industrial funding of long-term Arctic research in the years ahead may exceed that of government funding. If the existing Arctic projects designed by Canadian industry for the next few years go ahead as planned, one is looking at a possible total investment of over $5 billion. Even 2% of this sum devoted to environmental research would be a very significant sum. In addition, a considerable amount of Canadian public funds will soon be available for environmental research in the Arctic Ocean under the Environmental Studies Revolving Fund, which has recently been established pursuant to the Canada Oil and Gas Lands Act.

Reference was made to the current study of the Arctic Ocean "heat budget" as example of a long-term, high-priority, international research undertaking designed to provide knowledge in a seriously deficient area, which is expected to make important contributions to the scientific understanding of the world's climatic system. This kind of focus was chosen because of the spin-off benefits likely to be made available within such a comprehensive framework of investigations. With projects on this scale now under way, it can be seen that scientists are now moving up to a different level of understanding of the Arctic Ocean, after spending two decades or so on the same plateau.

The same speaker emphasized the need for Arctic scientists and administrators to look for cheaper ways of doing things. For example, more use could perhaps be made of small aircraft in field reseach, instead of relying in the traditional way on acquiring a research vessel. He concluded by emphasizing that this is a very exciting age for Arctic science. It is also a difficult period for Arctic biologists in particular, who may not even know what questions to ask, and almost certainly are denied the research time-scale that is necessary in order to deal effectively with the most critical scientific problems. Postponing the appropriate research, at the appropriate scale of investigation, is in nobody's long-term interest.

The next speaker commented on the new political complications in the life of a marine scientist, in the Arctic or elsewhere, which require permission to be secured, well in advance of the beginning of the research, from the nearest adjacent state. He feared that the need for Soviet permission and cooperation would prove to be a serious obstacle to future scientific research in the Arctic. He was more optimistic about future cooperation between government and industry in geological and engineering research on the continental shelf.

VII. ENVIRONMENTAL PRIORITIES

In introducing this topic, the panel chairman observed that the most significant alterations taking place in the marine environment are sometimes natural in origin, and not due to human activities. A great deal of attention is now being given to the phenomenon of climatic change in the North. Since the beginning of the present century the mean temperature of sub-Arctic waters has risen by 2° centigrade, but a slight cooling off has now begun. Climatic variation in the Arctic has important effects on the migration of certain species (such as Atlantic salmon and cod) and on the distribution of species in general. These variations are likely also to have discernible effects on the Northern island and coastal environments such as Greenland, Northern Norway, Iceland and Newfoundland. New research in climatic change was needed on a larger scale than in the past. Reference was also made to the need for increased research on the effects of oil spills in cold or ice-covered waters, and to the need for increased use of satellites as a research tool in Arctic environmental research.

The first invited speaker on environmental priorities described the existing environmental impact assessment procedures in Canada, which are now about 10 years old and in that time have dealt very with a number of Arctic projects. The Canadian approach to environmental assessment tends to be a compromise between the American and British approach: it is not directly designed as an integral component of the planning process as in the U.K., nor has it been developed in an institutionally and legally elaborate (and inflexible) way as in the United States. In Canada, under a Cabinet directive, all federal departments are required to take into account in the planning process the environmental implications of all new projects, programs, and activities involving federal lands or funding. Each federal ministry is responsible for determining whether its projects might result in "significant" environmental damage. If the risk of such damage seems sufficient, then a full-scale impact assessment study is necessary. In the early years the studies focused almost exclusively on the probable effects upon the natural environment, but more recently much more attention has been devoted to effects on the social environment. Originally, the review panels were composed wholly of federal bureaucrats. Now, the panels consist mostly of representatives from private sectors including special interest groups. A number of environmental impact assessment studies in Canada have been done in the North, where there is no possibility of federal-provincial conflict. Despite the political sensitivity of many such hearings, there is no evidence of Ministerial interference or influence. Indeed the process seems to have recently acquired a higher degree of credibility, especially since the postponement of the original Alaska Pipeline Project and the strict review of the current Lancaster Sound Project.

The Lancaster Sound Project experience, he continued, may reflect a changing focus for environmental impact assessment in Canada. The first assessment of this Project resulted in a recommendation for a broader review of all present and projected uses of Lancaster Sound in order to place the exploratory drilling for oil in a proper regional land-use planning perspective. This kind of reaction was certainly stronger, he said, than that of the review panels at the beginning of the process in the mid-1970's.

Some problems were of special concern, however. First, he observed, there is a serious insufficiency of technical expertise available for this kind of work in Canada. Part of the reason for this problem lies in the exodus of the appropriate expertise from government to the private sector, especially to the oil and gas industry. The question arising is "who is to assess the research". Second, there is the problem of native land claims, which complicate and aggravate the difficulties of environmental assessment. Sometimes the Inuit residents of the area refuse to participate in the review procedure, because of the fear that their participation might compromise their claim to part of the federal lands under review. When they do participate, their land claim tends to become another aspect of the overall environmental issue -- a political aspect which the technical expertise available is unqualified to deal with. Third, there is a problem of split jurisdictions and competing mandates. In the North, the Department of Indian and Northern Affairs (DINA) is the agency responsible for offshore developments; farther south, the matter falls under the jurisdiction of Energy, Mines and Resources (EMR). This has resulted in the anomalous situation that, whereas there has been a large-scale DINA-sponsored investigation for one single exploratory drill hole in Lancaster Sound, there has been no systematic environmental impact assessment for over 150 holes drilled in the offshore under the jurisdiction of EMR. Fourth, no one monitors the situation after a project has been reviewed and the panel has made its recommendations. As a result, no one knows whether the process is environmentally or cost effective. It is not even determined whether the Minister has acted upon the recommendations, much less whether they have been complied with in the execution of the project. Clearly, he said, it is impossible to know what beneficial environmental effect, if any, these procedures actually have.

In conclusion, it was suggested that a comparative study should be made of the costs and effectiveness of the U.S. and Canadian approaches. Such a study might also identify areas where a cooperative approach to environmental impact assessment could be undertaken by a joint body that would share experiences gained on both sides of the border. Such an initiative might be of special value in efforts to protect the Arctic Ocean environment: for example, in the Western Beaufort Sea, which is of interest to both countries.

The next speaker began by emphasizing the benefits as well as the costs of studying environmental risks associated with Arctic projects within a framework that encompassed the total Arctic Ocean system. The requirement to conduct environmental research within an ecosystemic framework underlined the inadequacy of our present knowledge; and it also pointed to the need for a degree of regional cooperation, since most of the ecosystems overlapped the jurisdictional boundaries. He advocated that special attention should be given to the changes being introduced in the river systems of the Arctic and to the effects of existing and proposed projects on the local areas.

The same speaker identified a number of environmental questions raised by the prospect of year-round shipping in the Arctic. For example, will navigation be facilitated or complicated by climatic change? Will shipping tracks tend to create thicker ice formations? Will the opening up of more free water in the summer affect the breeding patterns of marine mammals? Will the opening up of year-round shipping seriously disrupt the Inuit snowmobile routes (ice conditions too rugged in the winter, too much water in the summer)? What scientific evidence is likely to be available to provide an appropriate basis for the substitution of one shipping route for another?

He commented that the Arctic Waters Pollution Prevention Act is likely to continue to be a popular enactment in Canada, and to that extent represents a political opportunity to devise effective environmental regulations for shipping in the North. He hoped that the concern with specific pollution control techniques would not deflect environmentalists' attention from the larger scientific needs, such as that for the establishment of ecological reserves (specially protected areas) in the Arctic and other kinds of conservation initiatives. With this in mind he suggested that Northern Marine scientists should take a close look at the recent World Conservation Strategy as a possible framework for environmental planning under the concept of "eco-development". In conclusion, he referred to the need for closer integration between the physical and human elements of the Arctic environment in environmental planning and assessment applied to Arctic Ocean projects in the 1980's.

The following speaker emphasized the remarkable biological richness of the Lancaster Sound area, perhaps the most productive of any area at that latitude ("the Arctic equivalent of the Serengeti Valley in Kenya"). The special attention now being devoted to it was certainly justified scientifically. He also reminded the Workshop of the importance of the Lancaster Sound as a traditional hunting area for the native people of the region. Their life-style has been undergoing gradual modification for a century or more -- a much more gradual process of acculturation than in the Western Arctic -- but the projected developments in Lancaster Sound would constitute a different order of interference with their life- style.

Some concern was expressed about the possible harm to bird and mammal populations in Lancaster Sound as a result of the introduction of noise into that silent environment. Very little is known about the dynamics of these populations, but much may be learned from a current Man and the Biosphere (MAB) project on Arctic wildlife conservation. According to one participant, however, the local Inuit population is sometimes critical of international research effort being applied to such matters. Some Inuit were now proposing the development of "cooperative research" between professional scientists and the local community, whose observations and traditional knowledge of wildlife could have an important role within the framework of a scientific project. Another participant referred to the growing variety of sources of funding for environmental and conservation research, including industry and (in Alaska) the Inuit community.

To a question about the probable environmental effects of year-round shipping in the Arctic, one scientist replied that it was certainly fallacious to suppose that a major oil spill in the Arctic could have an appreciable effect on the world's climate, as some had suggested. (It seems unlikely that most oil spills in the Arctic could extend further than 10 square kilometers). Yet there is no doubt that temperature changes in the Arctic Ocean have a profound effect on global climatic patterns. Natural variations in the Arctic are probably greater than anything that could be induced by human activity, even with the significant increase in the atmosphere carbon dioxide load. The current Arctic heat budget is expected to shed further light on the validity or otherwise of the "instability theory" in Arctic climatology.

An American participant commented that it seemed that the Canadian scientific research effort in the Arctic in the years ahead would outdistance what American scientists were likely to be able to do in light of present and projected budgetary realities in the United States. In response, it was suggested that, with increased investment in Arctic scientific research, Canada would have to recruit some of the required expertise in the United States. It was unlikely that the Canadian Arctic research program of the 1980's could be carried out entirely by Canadian scientists.

VIII. EMERGING TECHNOLOGIES AND THE PROBLEM OF CHOICE

Dr. Ian R. McCallum opened this session with a presentation on the potentialities of the Cardiff ship simulator at the University of Wales Institute of Science and Technology and the South Glamorgan Institute of Higher Education (see his paper attached to this report). Special emphasis was placed on the utility of this research tool for those involved in developing ship systems in Arctic waters. He mentioned that efforts are being made to secure international cooperation in the acquisition of full-scale ship maneuvering data for general improvements in navigation techniques around the world. Reference was also made to simulator-aided research into the effects of stress on ship officers and crew, especially in difficult navigational conditions. Actual accidents have been re-run through the simulator with a view to discovering whether, and how, such collisions and strandings could have been avoided. He explained how the stranding of the Amoco Cadiz, for example, might have been avoided.

The next speaker, an engineer, opened by commenting on the importance of improving safety precautions for those who engage in engineering at sea. He underlined the priority attached to finding the appropriate construction materials to withstand stress, especially in Arctic waters in the presence of floating ice. One of the most serious difficulties experienced in Arctic engineering was the scarcity of reliable data. Many experimental methods of construction and operation are not yet fully developed for application to Arctic conditions. Indeed it was common for engineers to be asked to find practical solutions in the absence of adequate data. The art of feasibility studies was usually an exercise in approximation. Good engineers improvise: they have to "make do" with the best knowledge and equipment available.

The same speaker went on to compare some current engineering developments in the Northwest Atlantic offshore with similar developments in the Arctic Ocean. In both areas, he said, the costs of exploration and related activities are so high that unless the proposed methods are proved to be unsuitable in new conditions, their suitability is likely to be assumed and construction will proceed on that basis. Offshore engineering research is usually required to prove the technical unsuitability of a commercial proposal, which has already acquired a considerable degree of corporate support and perhaps already involved a significant amount of investment. It is often very difficult, technically, to prove that an alternative is clearly better.

He referred, for illustrative purposes, to the problem of drifting icebergs experienced in the course of Mobil's operations in the Hibernia area, and to the scouring of the seabed on the Grand Banks which was likely to rule out the use of pipelines. One suggested solution was to use a floating, detachable structure, but Mobil had not yet made a final decision on the type of technology to be used. For several years Dome had been looking for a floating system to be used in the Beaufort Sea, but this company was now investing in island structures for offloading. A "test island," a $50-100 million experiment, was referred to, as well as experiments directed at the use of superdredgers and ice-breaking tanks.

In the Eastern areas of the Northwest Passage, he reminded the Workshop, ice debris was more likely to be a shipping hazard than ice formation.

Reference was also made to engineering developments in the vicinity of Little Cornwallis Island, where mining activities were accelerating because of the high value of the local ore (27% metal). The entire refinery for this ore was being built on a barge, which would then be towed into the area and beached permanently in a hole, which has been blasted for that purpose. In this way it is hoped that the refinery will be sheltered from all ice movements in the vicinity. The chief environmental concern arises from the problem of disposal of the tailings at Garrow Lake, but recent research, it was suggested, has been relatively reassuring.

One participant questioned the acceptability of the "learning by doing" ethic in the Arctic Ocean, although it might be conceded that Dome had been rather successful in following that ethic. Pointing to the underlying policy dilemma over the allocation of risks and benefits in Arctic Ocean development, he expressed uneasiness over the present drilling program in the Beaufort Sea, given the absence of reliable information necessary for solving oil spill clean-up problems in unfavorable conditions. Unfortunately, he continued, the Canadian government had decided not to proceed with the development of the Class 10 ice-breaker for Canadian Coast Guard work in the Arctic, on the ground that it was too expensive. In its place, the Class 8 ice-breaker <u>may</u> be approved, but this might not be adequate for the kinds of activities planned for the late 1980's in the Western Arctic. A Class 10 ice-breaker was probably not necessary for transit through the Northwest Passage. The ice-breaker component of the Arctic Pilot Project is now being reconsidered.

Several alternative ice-breaking systems for the Arctic were compared. The merits of each approach depended on the set of assumptions that could validly be made regarding the kinds of activities and conditions involved. So far only a few, relatively minor, ice-related mishaps have occurred in the Beaufort Sea, but one could not discount the danger of a major spill through a blow-out or otherwise. One participant took the view that these risks might not be justifiable from a Canadian viewpoint, since Canada would not be dependent on the Beaufort oil for domestic consumption in the next 10 or 15 years. It might be better, he suggested, to postpone such risky explorations until better pollution control technology had been developed and commensurate benefits had become available. Another participant defended the Beaufort activities, which he regarded as useful in overcoming industrial and bureaucratic inertia in the context of Northern development.

Still another speaker conceded the difficulty, if not the impossibility, of determining the costs of certain kinds of environmental damage in the Arctic. Often the fears of ecological disaster in the region were exaggerated, even totally misplaced. But in contemplating the possible extinction of a rare Arctic species, one was talking of a loss of something irreplaceable: something of wonder on this planet. The major danger, he suggested, was of a major oil spill on the surface of the ice by a tanker in transit through the Northwest Passage -- near Leopold Island, for example. The ecological hazards rose not from the "fragility" of the environment, but from the fact that the different species of the Arctic Ocean were limited in number and yet occur in vast population concentrations. Dislocations in these areas of concentration, at certain times of the year, could be an extremely serious disruptive event within the ecosystem. There was nothing "trivial" about the deaths of millions of living creatures that might be left behind in the wake of a major oil spill in Arctic waters. And there was, unfortunately, a significant degree of probability that such an event might occur.

The appropriate response to these legitimate concerns, another speaker suggested, was the establishment and maintenance of the highest possible level of sophistication in a system of "transit management", not only in construction, design, and navigation standards but also in the standards applied to navigation aids, port requirements, and related shore-based facilities and procedures. But it would be difficult to design an appropriate system, at the required level of sophistication, without a clearer understanding of the future pattern of Arctic shipping movements than seemed to exist at present. For example, would the Northwest Passage be used for general cargo purposes as well as the transportation of Arctic resources?

To this another speaker replied that it was at least premature to talk of 1,000 Arctic Pilot Project voyages a year through the Northwest Passage. At present the Project was based on the use of only two ships, and each ship is presently scheduled to make 32 round trips each year through the Passage. He agreed however, that an expanded version of the Arctic Pilot Project, in combination with other projects (e.g., transportation of Beaufort Sea and Arctic islands oil and other minerals), could raise the level of shipping movements through the Passage to close to 500 voyages (i.e., 1,000 transits) by the year 2000. He agreed also on the critical importance of adequate ice-breaking support for navigation through the Passage. So far there had been fairly good cooperation between Canadian government and Canadian industry in preparing for the future regulation of Arctic shipping, but it was admittedly still a rudimentary stage in the development of "ice management" in these waters. A good deal had been learned recently from the experience of port managers in the Baltic.

After further discussion, it was generally agreed that "aggressive" Canadian legislation was needed to establish an acceptably rigorous system of "transit management" in the Northwest Passage. Only the highest possible standards, several contended, should be regarded as "acceptable" for this uniquely risky waterway. It was noted that under Article 234 of the Draft Convention on the Law of the Sea Canada would have a very wide area of almost unqualified authority in the development and application of vessel traffic management controls in the Northwest Passage. Such authority would extend to design, construction, manning and equipment standards for foreign and domestic vessels alike, as well as to discharge and navigational practices. Particular attention should be given to the design of special training courses for mariners authorized to navigate in ice-covered waters. Even now, it was observed, special training requirements were being considered for officers and crew to be engaged in the carriage of LNG under the Arctic Pilot Project.

In joining the discussion of the precautions required for navigation control in the Passage, one scientist began by suggesting that oil was not the most serious pollution hazard in the Arctic. The most appropriate response to environmental hazards associated with the new Arctic technologies, he continued, would be the introduction of a system for continuous monitoring of the Arctic Ocean environment. This was likely to be a more effective approach than the most elaborate environmental impact assessment studies. In reply, it was pointed out that Petro-Canada, like British Petroleum, now has a well-established monitoring program. Another commentator agreed that monitoring was essential, not as a substitute for environmental impact assessment, but as a necessary follow-up after the fact. All Northern developments are, in effect, experimental in character, but the assessments themselves should be assessed. At present, he reiterated, even the best prepared assessments in Canada are of little predictive value, as long as there are no systematic efforts to conduct follow-up investigation. There seemed to be too few incentives at present for government to go back and re-examine earlier studies and recommendations. Another commentator suggested that the chief purpose of environmental assessment was political rather than scientific: to curtail fears and "manage" discontent rather than to validate hypotheses. In Alaska, another observed, three years seemed to be about the longest period for any Arctic monitoring project to date, and this was not nearly enough for most scientific purposes. Another conceded that government regulations, like corporate policies, tend to be myopic in the field of environmental impact. The primary focus tends to be on social effects, not scientific significance. The tendency was to give priority to the reduction of criticism and resistance. On the whole, government tends to be even more guilty of this than industry.

The participants seemed to be generally in agreement that the choice of technology and the assessment of future technological impacts in the Arctic Ocean were unlikely to become entirely objective or rational processes. Both the exaggeration and the neglect of threats to wildlife -- to migratory species in the Beaufort Sea, for example -- were the product of emotional, subjective judgments, rather than of the professional opinions of unbiased biologists. Yet it was possible and important for government to specify the operating conditions for industry wishing to exploit resources in a threatened environment.

A political scientist noted that environmental management was complicated, almost everywhere, by the conflict of expert testimony among scientists called upon to provide "adversary evidence." Rules for management have to be standardized, by lawyers and public administrators. Once a standard is set up within a rigid system of uniform rules, it becomes exceedingly difficult to change it as new knowledge comes in. The case of the recent ban on swordfishing was referred to by way of illustration.

Another speaker returned to the prediction of voyages through the Northwest Passage. Sticking to his earlier contention, he asserted that the next phase of the Arctic Pilot Project could, quite conceivably, involve as many as 30 vessels. If each of these vessels was able to undertake 30 such voyages (15 return trips) each year, then 1,000 passages per year by the year 2000 (or 1995) seemed to be a distinct possibility.

One of the scientists, responding to a question about the relative seriousness of oil spills in the Arctic Ocean, said that if there has to be an oil spill, it might be better to have it under ice rather than in clear water, since the ice cover would tend to control the spread and reduce the scope of potential ecological damage in the surrounding area.

IX. THE PATTERN OF CORPORATE INITIATIVES

The principal speaker began by reminding the Workshop that if all industrial Arctic projects now under consideration in North America were to go ahead as scheduled, the total investment involved in the next five years might be in excess of $5 billion. Then the same speaker proceeded to describe the current pattern of activities of oil companies in the North American Arctic.

At the western extreme of the North American Arctic, ARCO and BP/SOHIO have been active on the North Slope for a number of years. Much of their work has been innovative and living conditions have been raised to a fairly high level on an unprecedented scale of development activity. Their environmental research has been impressive, and soon other U.S. oil companies will be joining in these operations on the Slope.

Further eastwards, Dome Petroleum is gearing up fast for the production and transportation of oil and natural gas from the Beaufort Sea. Dome has been engaged in exploratory drilling here since 1976. It is not yet known whether commercial quantities have been discovered, but the rapid rate of exploration seems to reflect a high degree of confidence. Dome, unlike most Arctic entrepreneurs, started from scratch, and has been "learning by doing" on site, acquiring technological virtuosity on the job. Dome's approach, dependent on the use of drill ships, has required a willingness on the part of this company to build its own ships specifically for work in Arctic conditions.

In adjacent areas of the Beaufort Sea, Gulf and Esso Resources have begun drilling from artificial islands -- another form of technology that has proved highly successful.

A little farther north, in the northeast corner of Canada Basin and in the Melville Island area, Pan-Arctic has found gas. The plan, in conjunction with the Arctic Pilot Project, is to pipe that gas down from the top of Melville Island to Bridport Inlet in the south of Melville Island, to liquefy it there in a floating barge plant and then transfer the LNG in specially designed tankers through the Northwest Passage and southward through Baffin Bay and Davis Strait to a southern re-gasification terminal to be located either in the Strait of Canso in Nova Scotia or at a Gulf of St. Lawrence locality in Quebec.

The entrance to Baffin Bay from Lancaster Sound is a promising structure, and Petro-Canada has conducted extensive environmental and engineering design studies with a view to the feasibility of future drilling, but unfortunately this area overlaps with an area of considerable biological importance. Further south in Baffin Bay, between Baffin Island and the west of Greenland, a number of companies have been engaged in exploratory drilling, but so far these efforts have not been successful. A little further south in Davis Strait drilling has been carried out by Aquitaine and Imperial.

The same speaker also referred to mining activities at Nanasivik on Borden Peninsula, Baffin Island, the "Polaris" mining site on Little Cornwallis Island north of Barrow Strait. The lead-zinc ore from these sites will be shipped out through Lancaster Sound and Baffin Bay to markets in Western Europe, as soon as they are found to be minable in commercial quantities. Petro-Canada and other companies are looking for coal in a number of areas, such as Ellesmere Island in the far north. Reference was also made to uranium prospects.

In the sub-Arctic area further south, off Labrador, British Petroleum, Chevron, Aquitaine, Imperial, Petro-Canada, Total-Eastran and a number of other companies are, or have been, active in exploration for offshore petroleum resources. Eventually, one reaches the area of greatest mineral promise on and beyond the Grand Banks of Newfoundland.

Oil discoveries in the Arctic Ocean are all tentative so far (except on the North Slope), but hopes are fairly high especially in the Beaufort Sea. Natural gas discoveries, on the other hand, are significant in quantity, but of course these gas reserves are not so badly needed. Even if the highest petroleum hopes materialized in the North American Arctic, they might still be less than the proven reserves of Mexico -- and a tiny fraction of the not-yet-attainable minerals in the Athabasca Tar Sands of Alberta. Coal, not oil or gas, may prove to be the chief Arctic mineral resource of the future, if one looks beyond the next ten years.

X. CONCLUSIONS

1. Supplementary Matters. In this final session the participants ranged over the entire spectrum of current developments and issues discussed earlier in in the Workshop with a view to establishing a "synthesis", if not a consensus, of views on Arctic Ocean policy priorities for the 1980's.

The first speaker wished to add certain points of importance that had not received sufficient emphasis. For instance, biologists are still a bit puzzled about the levels of primary production in several areas, especially Hudson Bay. Hudson Bay has repeatedly been described as low in productivity, but this may now be open to revision. For one thing, such primary production measurements as have been made in Hudson Bay have been made too late in the season to measure the peak of the phytoplankton bloom. Secondary production (200 plankton) seems to be reasonably high and although there are no commercially exploitable populations of fish, the sea mammals are plentiful, and the whalers years ago expressed astonishment at the abundance of large whales, which they proceeded to overkill.

On a time scale somewhat longer than legal and political scholars normally take into account, the age of the polar ecosystems is probably important. The contrast between the levels of biological productivity and ecosystem development in the North and those in the Southern (Antarctic) Ocean, where sea mammals and krill are so plentiful, may well be due to the different ages of the two systems. The Antarctic glaciation started some millions of years (perhaps between 15 and 20 million years) before the Arctic glaciation, so that the Southern ecosystem is better adapted to polar conditions than the younger system in the North. Hudson Bay is even younger than much of the Arctic Ocean and adjacent seas.

The same speaker, in response to a question, discussed the possibility of introducing new or alien species into Arctic waters. Pacific salmon had been introduced into western areas of Hudson Bay, but this experiment had not been successful. It was particularly difficult to effect a successful introduction of an anadromous species like the salmon, with a slow growth and reproduction cycle and long-range migratory requirements. Since salmon had always thrived in Ungava Bay nearby, it did not seem that water temperature was a critical factor. Char, another anadromous species, was everywhere throughout the Arctic, but its vulnerability to overfishng by the local communities had limited the possibility of developing char fisheries at a commercial level.

Another speaker commented further on the military (strategic) significance of the Arctic Ocean. He put forward the view that the waters and islands of the Arctic region were unlikely to become a critical component of offensive systems. Soviet offensive systems would probably be air-based, and U.S. missile (ABM) and submarine facilities need not depend heavily on Arctic Ocean bases. But there was little doubt that, defensively, the Soviet Union regarded itself as vulnerable in the Arctic, especially in view of the importance of Murmansk as its chief naval base. Increasing industrial activity off Northern Norway must be expected to make the Russian strategic planners even more sensitive. In response to the suggestion that the Arctic was the soft underbelly of the Soviet Union, he contended that the Soviet Union was likely to be even more concerned about the threat in the Eastern Mediterranean: all strategically important places in the country were south of Moscow. Further discussion revealed a difference of views on the potential strategic value of the Arctic seabed. With or without reference to the specific role of the Arctic in defense matters, it seemed at least that a new approach to U.S.-Canadian cooperation in defense was timely, if not overdue. Meanwhile, Canadian sovereignty sensitivities were likely to continue to be aroused by the unauthorized transit of U.S. submarines in Canadian Arctic waters.

2. The Basic Questions. In introducing the final phase of the Workshop, devoted to the task of "synthesis", the panel chairman reviewed the range of questions that had already been raised and discussed. He suggested that the following in particular might be regarded as the most pertinent.

First, how should we perceive the institutional deficiencies of the Arctic as a region? Does the Arctic Ocean, or some part of it, need a "regime"? If so, what kind of regime? Several different kinds serving different "functional" purposes? Or one all-encompassing, "general purposes" regime?

If separate, must they be parallel or compatible with one another? If there should be Arctic Ocean regimes, which states should (or must) be included? Should there be bilateral or only multilateral regimes? Should the "Soviet link" be preserved within such regimes? If so, for what kinds of purposes? Should Canada and the Nordic states resort to their own arrangements in the region, independently of the two Arctic superpowers?

Second, as to development -- the engine of change in the North --how important is it? How critical is the energy reserve in the Arctic Ocean likely to be? Which minerals in the North will prove to be the most valuable by the end of the century? What risks are we prepared to take, what sacrifices are we willing to make, in order to secure the most valuable of these resources?

Third, how important is Arctic Ocean research, compared with other areas of research? To what extent are we compelled, should we be driven, by scientific curiosity? How far is Arctic Ocean research likely to be dictated by short-term industrial -- or even short-term "national" -- interest considerations? What are the prospects of appropriately long-term, appropriately large-scale, research in the Arctic Ocean? Are effective research projects in the region likely to remain dependent on vessel-based activities, or will non-vessel modes of technology be used increasingly as substitute procedures? In what sectors of research is international coordination or cooperation -- with or without extra-regional institutions -- essential to effective scientific inquiry?

Fourth, in environmental matters how are the relevant costs and benefits to be weighed in the balance? What, precisely, are the environmental priorities in the Arctic Ocean? How great are the hazards now in contemplation? How much environmental cooperation can we realistically expect between government, industry, local community, and special interest group? Is Soviet (and U.S.) research essential to effective environmental management of the Canadian Arctic waters?

Fifth, on matters related to the Northwest Passage, how sensitive is the question of Canadian sovereignty (or exclusive management authority)? What are the actual requirements for effective management in these waters? Is a complete "transit management" approach essential? What is involved in the establishment and maintenance of a sophisticated and effective system of this kind? How much discretion must be left to Canada as the "manager" of the Passage? What is the appropriate scale of investment in navigational aids, ice-breakers, and other physical facilities? What kinds of special regulations are needed? What special enforcement and surveillance techniques should be employed? What range of sanctions should be envisaged? Will Canadian waters in the Arctic be treated as cabotage areas, limited to vessels of Canadian registry, by analogy with Canadian coastal trading areas in the South?

Finally, what do we want to happen in the Arctic Ocean? What do we want <u>not</u> to happen?

3. <u>Regionalism and Regimes</u>. The first commentator on the questions regarding regionalism and regimes began by holding to his contention that the Arctic is indeed a region, not only in the physical sense but also in a more meaningful way for Inuit and scientists. He conceded that the Arctic has not yet become fully developed as a political region, but pointed to political developments that seem to reflect a trend toward regionalization. In particular, he emphasized the need to produce selective Arctic regional policy in matters conducive to cooperation among the circumpolar nations, such as scientific research and environmental protection. He was inclined to discourage an Arctic or Arctic Ocean focus in arms control policy-making (which would simply aggravate Soviet sensitivities in the region) or indeed in any other context likely to be dominated by exogenous considerations. The smaller ice-states should perhaps lead the way in taking the first steps toward <u>selective</u> regional integration in the Arctic. He conceded that total pan-Arctic cooperation was not feasible at present, even for environmental purposes, but felt that current trends in Arctic transportation and resource development would eventually draw the Soviet Union in to some kind of functional regime, for reasons similar to those that have operated in the Arctic.

The second commentator took the view that it is not necessary to look at the Arctic as a political region in the foreseeable future, and confessed to having some doubts also about the desirability of political integration in the Arctic in the longer term. However desirable for certain scientific purposes it seemed impossible to anticipate the emergence of any kind of pan-Arctic institutional framework. In the Soviet Union the decision whether or not to participate in such a body would be made by strategists, not by scientists. Increased vessel movements in the Arctic Ocean, whether for research or commercial purposes, would be interpreted negatively from their national security perspective. He maintained that the sector principle should be taken seriously as a basis of Soviet action, whatever the validity of such a claim in the doctrine of international law. A partial, functional regime for climate research purposes might be feasible, perhaps with the Russians cooperating on an associate, non-member basis, but he felt that a more widely defined scientific regime was unlikely to have Soviet participation.

The same speaker reminded the Workshop of the vast difference between American and Canadian perceptions of the

Arctic. He did not think that the present or foreseeable pattern of interactions among the circumpolar nations was such as to require them to look at the Arctic as an evolving political region. Nor did he see any serious problems emerging that seemed incapable of solution under existing or <u>ad hoc</u> bilateral arrangements. He did not believe that the United States should have a higher priority in the Arctic, but emphasized that the U.S. government develop a higher awareness of Canadian sensitivities in that region, in any context that impinged on U.S.-Canadian relations.

The third commentator, also American, agreed essentially with the previous speaker. He reiterated that there was no compelling reason for the United States to develop a strategic perspective specifically on the Arctic, but in conceding that some existing strategic regimes (e.g. outer space and seabed) contributed at least symbolically to the cause of world peace, he agreed that the Arctic Ocean might, in the years ahead, provide a "reasonable excuse" for the United States and the Soviet Union to sit down, with or without other nations, to negotiate an Arctic Ocean counterpart regime. It might be assumed that within five years or less some kind of effort will be initiated within the United Nations to secure international control over certain resources (beyond the continental margin) in the Arctic Ocean, in a region that some might wish to regard as an international area. Such an effort, he argued, would depend on the level of Third World dissatisfaction with resource diplomacy outcomes after UNCLOS III and in other forums. He closed with the suggestion that an U.S.-Canadian Arctic Ocean arrangement of some kind might be useful as a new opening in U.S.-Canadian relations.

4. <u>Resource Development</u>. The first speaker on this subject emphasized that the Arctic water and land areas about to receive the impact of industrial development must be perceived as a region at the sub-national level at least. In an area that must be studied carefully for purposes of regional development and planning it will be necessary to take account of the rights and claims of the native peoples. Until these claims are settled -- hopefully within the next five years or so -- it is very difficult to assess the impact of resource development on the communities of the North.

The next commentator observed that there is now no question <u>whether</u> the Arctic will be developed. It is a question of <u>how</u> and what precautionary safety measures should be taken to ensure that development has the most beneficial effects on the communities and natural environment of the North? The focus now should be on the design and development of an appropriate managerial or regulatory infrastructure, not least with a view to the prospect of regular, year-round transit through the Northwest Passage.

Another participant pointed out that developmental planning is now being initiated in this multinational region despite some basic uncertainties about the structure of government that may exist there in 10 or 20 years. By then the Canadian territories may -- or may not -- have provincial status. Even with statehood, many Alaskans today are still dissatisfied with their position in the American governmental system and talk of the need for some kind of structural adjustment. The recently acquired home rule status of Greenland is having a profound and complicating effect on industrial development planning in the Eastern Arctic. By the year 2000, Greenland might be as independent of Danish influence as, say, Iceland is today. The aspirations of the Lapp people of Norway, Sweden and Finland might be projected into some new form of semi-autonomous or wholly autonomous association across the existing boundaries of these countries by the early years of the 21st century.

Another speaker raised the idea of some kind of joint approach to resource development on the continental shelf beyond 200 mile limits of national (economic zone) jurisdiction. Roughly speaking, the 200 mile zones in the Arctic Ocean encompass something like 5 million square miles of water area, leaving an "enclave" of perhaps one million square miles beyond in the middle of the Arctic Ocean basin. Even though most of that enclave may come under national jurisdiction, by virtue of the new UNCLOS III definition of the continental shelf, there may still be merit in the idea of a joint development strategy on the part of two or more neighboring littoral Arctic states. A scientist replied that there may be all sorts of valuable resources within the enclave, or at least on the shelves of the enclave. He pointed out that the International Biological Programme (IBP), like the International Geological Year (IGY) before it, had attracted a good deal of scientific interest to the Arctic High.

5. Scientific Research. It was found difficult to deal directly with the question concerning the value of Arctic science. There is no way of measuring the value of science objectively. One participant thought that the key questions related to the appropriate level of investment in scientific research and to the direction of scientific inquiry. Another suggested that the focus should be on the uses of science both negatively in the generation of conflict and positively in the resolution of conflict. But there are also "why" questions to be addressed concerning the various purposes of Arctic science before research investment priorities can be set.

Certainly one of the crucial issues in science policy generally, and Arctic science policy in particular, it was agreed, is the relationship between bureaucracy and science. Both the scientists and the non-scientists participating in this discussion were divided on the question of how to evaluate the consequences of bureaucratic involvement in Arctic science. At least it was generally agreed that, whether for good or ill, governmental and industrial priorities were the primary determinant of the present and anticipated patterns of scientific research in the Arctic Ocean. To that extent Arctic science was a "closed system". Several argued from this that the future of Arctic research might be much more selective than it should be. One commentator suggested that the acid rain problem in North America had remained neglected so long mainly because the "closed system" of governmental and industrial research had failed to support certain areas of inquiry such as atmospheric chemistry which could have provided the appropriate warnings decades ago.

Another speaker questioned whether the "closed system" in the Arctic was in fact having the effect of deflecting inquiry from the fundamental areas. The present emphasis on the Arctic "heat budget" was clearly defensible: it represented a unique opportunity to acquire important information required in the field of climatology, a matter of concern to virtually every nation in the world. Moreover, almost all research activities in the Arctic -- from oil spill research, through ice movement studies, to the study of migratory patterns -- are relevant to heat budget research.

Several scientists present denied that any of the scientific topics listed at the Workshop were merely "nice" or "interesting": each, properly viewed, was an essential piece of the Arctic Ocean "jig-saw puzzle". Each should be pursued now, even if some may not seem to have an immediate "practical" value. Sooner or later everything may be understood to have such a value directly or indirectly. The general purpose of all science is to raise our understanding to the point that "value judgments" of that kind can be made more intelligently. To that extent, there was a sense in which science should drive the "system" rather than the other way around, but realistically the money had to be provided from somewhere within the "system" of government and industry.

At this stage of the Workshop three distinct Arctic science policy concerns had surfaced. First, some participants believed that the "closed system" of Arctic research was not at present unduly confining, but conceded that it required constant monitoring from outside as well as inside for basic moral reasons. Science could, and sometimes did, result in the generation rather than the resolution of conflict, and all human values were subordinate, ultimately, to the maintenance of world peace. Second, another group was genuinely concerned, even alarmed, over the prospect of a "closed system" of Arctic Ocean research dominated by relatively short-term governmental and industrial priorities. The fact that the system was "closed" made it extremely difficult for those on the outside to carry out effective monitoring. Even in areas where institutional procedures for environmental impact assessment had been established, there was no provision for meaningful follow-up, monitoring studies to assess the effectiveness, if any, of these procedures. Third, several of the American participants were seriously disturbed by the erosion of U.S. federal government support for Arctic research, and by the lack of any serious effort to coordinate related research activities under conditions of scarcity.

One scientist pointed out that one or two of the most prominent industrial (corporate) supporters of Arctic Ocean research today are now prepared to place such research on a 10-20 year basis, which is a longer time-frame than is normally possible under government auspices. But industrial Arctic research is more suspect in some countries than in others. The recently established Comite Arctique in Monaco -- an international, nongovernmental, scientific organization -- might be an appropriate mechanism to stimulate industrial support of Arctic research without the constraints that characterize the "closed system". On the one hand, industry seems to see the Comite Arctique as a convenient forum for the exchange of scientific information without involvement in the problems associated with the regulatory process. On the other hand, the organization provides an intermediary between industry and government, facilitating the use of industrial funds for Arctic research of interest to governments which cannot, for political reasons, accept research grants directly from industrial sources.

Several speakers referred to the continuing involvement of national security (including military) inputs into the design of U.S. science policy. There is no prospect that this will change in the near future. Moreover, the future of U.S. oceanography in particular is at present extremely obscure, and "not amenable to short-run manipulation" for Arctic or any other specific purposes. A Canadian observed that official U.S. scientific cooperation with the Soviet Union in this area remains unlikely as long as a major portion of U.S. Arctic and oceanographic research continues to be funded by the military. If American Arctic scientists wish to achieve significant cooperation with their Russian counterparts, they will have to make greater use of industrial funding and unofficial linkages -- as a necessary, if not sufficient, condition for cooperation in Arctic research.

One American speaker indicated that there is some evidence that the pendulum may be swinging back in favor of more U.S. Arctic research, because of the need to get more specific information about certain uses of the Arctic Ocean. Another pointed out American Arctic scientists had become overly dependent on ice-breaking vessels, and had to design their research activities to conform with the movements of such vessels. It was noted that the logistical situation was not quite so bad in Canada, where Arctic scientists normally had relatively easy access to government vessels, but American scientists needed very badly an ice-strengthened research vessel which could be used for year-round research in both polar regions.

6. Environmental Protection. The first commentator on this subject began by re-emphasizing the need to strengthen the existing coalition of interests involved in environmental impact assessment work in Canada. The long-term opportunities to improve the quality and utility of impact assessment in the North are good, because we are virtually starting from scratch. But the most serious flaw in current assessment work -- the lack of predictive value -- is intellectual rather than institutional. He contrasted this general deficiency in environmental impact assessment with the specific knowledge that had been gained in studies of the environmental effects of dams and irrigation improvements. Over the last 100 years approximately 4,000 man-made dams have been constructed around the world. Because of the concentration of biological and other scientific expertise that has developed around these projects, it is now possible to predict, in general terms, what happens to a moving body of water when it is dammed up. This knowledge exists only because of the amount of research that has been devoted to monitoring the physical, chemical and biological changes which occur in a reservoir over an extended time period. Information of this kind has become available for consideration in the design and construction of more recent dams. Comparable success in the design and construction of Arctic Ocean development projects is impossible without a similar effort to obtain the necessary "after the fact" information. As matters now stand, Canadian environmental impact assessment studies in the Arctic Ocean serve, at best, limited and short-term pollution prevention and abatement purposes. We must find a way of making a reasonable estimate of what is likely to occur in potentially vulnerable project areas such as Lancaster Sound. (Approval for drilling in the Davis Strait was granted only after a good ecological study had been carried out, but this was a less threatened area). After properly based predictions have been made, a serious effort must be made to ensure the maintenance of post-approval monitoring.

The next speaker, an American, underlined that the Canadian authorities, in designing an environmental protection regime for the Northwest Passage, should take into account the international nature of the interest in transit through these difficult waters. He suggested that it would be unnecessarily provocative for the Canadian government to assert a sovereignty basis for such a management regime, when it is open to it to maintain its present "functional" posture in its jurisdictional claims to the Arctic Ocean. As to possible American initiatives in the environmental protection of the Beaufort Sea, he suggested that special institutional arrangements were needed, perhaps within a system of "special geographical areas" that could be designated by the U.S. National Academy of Sciences.

The next speaker expressed his concern that environmental research was conceived too narrowly. What was desirable was a more clearly perceived linkage between research effort and the predictable consequences of industrial development. Certain kinds of research should be supported by industry, because of the long-term value it would have for dealing with development problems: for example, research in the field of climatic change might have a direct bearing, in the long run, on the costs of transportation in the Arctic Ocean. Research into the disposal of tailings from mining operations in the region might be viewed in the same light.

There was some general discussion about the appropriate emphasis in a system of environmental monitoring for the Arctic Ocean. A truly comprehensive monitoring system would be very expensive to establish and maintain. Some kind of special emphasis would have to be designed into it, especially if it was to be continued indefinitely. Arguably, a monitoring program should be designed mainly along biological lines. Davis Strait was suggested as a suitable focus for the monitoring of migrations, and of course Lancaster Sound for the monitoring of oil spills. Although the oil pollution hazard in the Arctic Ocean may now appear to be less severe than was feared ten years ago, from the point of view of oil spill spread and clean-up difficulties in ice-covered waters, oil could certainly cause serious damage to the Arctic Ocean food chain, and this would justify the special attention of an environmental monitoring program. Oil pollution in the Arctic had not become a "straw man", as some earlier speakers had suggested.

Another speaker confirmed that the pollution hazard was taken seriously in the oil industry itself. Indeed the oil companies now were conducting a significant amount of Arctic research because of these concerns. The fragility of the Arctic marine environment may have been overstated by some alarmists in the past, but oil pollution research is now a major activity under the auspices of the Arctic Petroleum Operators Association (APDA). Every year the Canadian APDA, and its research affiliate, the Canadian offshore Oil Spill Research Association (COOSRA), meet with the U.S. Arctic Beaufort Sea Oilspill Research Body (ABSORB). In Canada, it was pointed out, there is fairly close consultation between APDA/COOSRA and the oil spill research staff of the Environmental Protection Service of Environment Canada.

Another speaker, an international lawyer, referred to recent efforts around the world to produce regional cooperation in the protection of the marine environment. The Regional Seas Programme of UNEP (United Nations Environment Programme) was described as one approach that had had considerable success in attracting government support through the adoption of an Action Plan and treaty instruments for the various regional seas designated under the Programme. But this globally conceived Programme was not designed for a regional sea like the Arctic Ocean. In some respects a pan-regional, but more limited approach to environmental marine management in a "developed" region like the Baltic Sea might be regarded as being closer to a model for the Arctic Ocean, if political realities were to permit any mode of intergovernmental cooperation in environmental protection. Surely an extremely limited, _ad hoc_, selective arrangement like the Polar Bear Convention did not represent the "end of the line" in Arctic environmental cooperation.

The general consensus seemed to be, however, that environmental issues in the Arctic Ocean were not yet sufficiently acute as an _international_ problem, to impel the governments of the region into any kind of political arrangement based on the Baltic or Mediterranean models.

7. _Legal Issues_. The first commentator on this topic, an American, reminded the Workshop of the gap between Canadian and U.S. perceptions of the legal issues of the Arctic Ocean. In Canada the sovereignty sentiment was still a powerful emotional current in Arctic policy thinking, whereas the U.S. government was content to leave most Arctic issues at a low level of national priority. If it was true that the United States could approach these issues in a relatively pragmatic spirit, then it represented an opportunity for American diplomacy to find ways fo resolving U.S.-Canadian differences in Arctic policy without aggravating existing tensions. He suggested it might be timely to introduce some kind of "cooperative institution" in Arctic affairs that would be detached to some extent from the political or diplomatic level of Canadian-U.S. relations.

The second speaker, also American, felt that it would be unwise for Canada to inject Arctic issues into any context of trade-off diplomacy, whether bilateral or multilateral. This approach had worked fairly well for Canada at UNCLOS III in very special global circumstances, but in the future it might be safer for the Canadian government to deal with Arctic Ocean matters directly on their merits. The global implications of the Arctic Ocean, he added, were minimal under the new law of the sea. The continental margin in the Arctic Ocean extended, in places, as far as 350 miles from the shore, leaving a rather insignificant area of seabed in the middle of the Arctic Ocean basin that might be regarded as "international". The prospects of extracting resources from that area were extremely remote, and it was simply not worth the "hassle" that would be involved in confronting the legal issues inherent in any effort to secure access to them.

The following speaker, a Canadian, speculated on two types of Canadian Arctic Ocean legislation that might be expected in the wake of UNCLOS III. First, one should anticipate economic zone legislation designed to assert Canadian sovereign rights over the resources falling under the new zone and to implement Canadian controls over pollution risks from vessel and non-vessel sources. Within this kind of legislative framework one should expect to see the development of detailed regulations governing transit throught the Northwest Passage, as contemplated in Article 234 of the Draft Convention on the Law of the Sea. Second, after the resolution of outstanding boundary disputes with the United States and Denmark, Canada can be expected to promulgate its Arctic Ocean boundaries in legislative form. Theoretically, it might be possible for Canada to promulgate Arctic baselines before these disputes are settled -- and to promulgate the seaward limits of its continental shelf in the Arctic under Article 76 -- but in practice it is difficult to see what would be gained in the short term by doing so. The establishment of a management system for the Northwest Passage does not seem to depend on the enactment of legislation of this latter kind.

Another legal specialist began by referring to the "preferential" regimes that Canada and the Soviet Union had developed in the Arctic Ocean in the face of actual or anticipated pressures from other countries. These Canadian and Soviet efforts had very largely succeeded in carving out vast areas of virtually exclusive control for these claimant coastal states. He expressed scepticism, however, that the principle of Article 234 (the "ice-covered exception") could be regarded as established in customary international law, as matters now stand. Prior to general adoption of the entire UNCLOS III, he was doubtful that any one part of the package could be singled out and upheld as legally binding. Provisional consent by national delegations for purposes of negotiation at a law-making conference was certainly not the same thing as consent in state practice.

As to whether there are ways of proceeding, unilaterally or bilaterally, with Arctic development in the absence of a binding Convention on the Law of the Sea, he thought at least that the opening up of the Northwest Passage would have a "remarkable effect" on the shaping of Soviet policy in the Arctic Ocean, especially if it happened before the opening up of the Northeast Passage in the Soviet Arctic. Such a situation might force the Soviets to reconsider their present nationalistic policy in the Arctic in order to avoid suffering a competitive disadvantage internationally in developmental terms.

Questioned about the Soviet sector theory, the same speaker said that Soviet authorities had been careful in recent years to refrain from making any sector claim in the strictly jurisdictional sense, and also in the political sense of a "sphere of influence". This did not mean, of course, that they would feel precluded from making either type of claim in the future, if they felt it was imperative to protect a vital national interest in the region. It should be understood that the sector theory in the narrow jurisdictional sense would hinder, not help, Soviet scientific research in the Arctic Ocean.

The following commentator, a Canadian, agreed that the sector theory (in the legal sense) should be buried once and for all, and that this view was certainly shared by Soviet jurists. He disagreed, however, with the previous speaker's comments on the status of Article 234 in customary international law. In recent years customary international law has "jelled" much more quickly than 20-25 years ago. Indeed the International Court of Justice has recognized that the concept of the continental shelf had become established swiftly in customary international law after 1945.

Canada, he continued, had three sets of interests to protect in the Arctic Ocean: the natural environment, the local population, and a national security interest. The threats to these interests in the Northwest Passage come from two main sources: navigation (especially the transportation of oil and gas and the passage of military vessels) and the exploitation of mineral rights at the entrance to Lancaster Sound. In his view, Canada had no alternative but to do the best it can to secure full control over these activities threatening Canadian interests in the Northwest Passage. It is not, of course, easy to suggest how this might be best accomplished, though it should be possible to work out some kind of agreement with the United States: some kind of coastal state/user state agreement, whereby Canada would guarantee the transit of U.S. vessels through the Passage in return for U.S. recognition of Canadian management authority over these waters. He did not believe, he added, in a special legal or political regime for the Arctic Ocean, except for the existing UNCLOS III-sanctioned regime of special coastal state competence in the environmental management in ice-covered waters under Article 234. Although he did not believe in the so-called sector doctrine, it might be convenient to use the sectoral method of delineating geographical areas within which the coastal states would have special administrative responsibility for purposes of environmental protection.

Another Canadian participant agreed with an earlier speaker that it was in the interest of Canada and the Soviet Union to avoid making formal sovereignty-type claims, but to "fill in the picture", as the need arose, with functionally defined, clearly distinguished, legislative measures. In the same spirit of non-confrontation, an American speaker felt it would be in neither Canada's nor America's interest to deny or to assert, loudly and publicly, that the Northwest Passage was an international strait. The issue could be finessed quite appropriately through the kind of Canadian-U.S. accommodation referred to earlier.

8. Operational Requirements. The chief commentator on this topic began by emphasizing the importance of introducing sound operational standards and procedures into Arctic navigation. Because of the complete lack of habitation in the area, shipping control would be especially difficult to bring into effect in the Northwest Passage. A register of qualified vessels -- those approved as suitable for Arctic navigation -- should be opened, and the criteria for qualification should be clearly set out. "Transit management" in the region would require a system of effective monitoring over the entire length of the projected seaway: an area of approximately 1,000 miles. The monitoring would have to be effected by aircraft patrols or shore-based radar stations. Compulsory reporting by approaching vessels would be another feature of a proper vessel traffic management system. Since failures can be expected to be common and difficult in such conditions, provision will have to be made for back-up (towing and repair) services, and these will be expensive to maintain in the region. The rules will have to be numerous and tough if a rigorous management system is to be effective. There will also have to be a serious determination by Canadian authorities to enforce the rules, and this too will add considerably to the cost of operation. All of these measures have been adopted by France and the United Kingdom in the English Channel, admittedly in less arduous circumstances. It is difficult to believe that anything less than this can be adequate in the Northwest Passage.

An American participant commented that he did not have any difficulty with an operational system of that kind for the Northwest Passage. This would be consistent with his conception of a waterway available for international use subject to appropriate rules applied by the coastal state, provided that it was not accompanied by an assertion of sovereignty.

Reference was made to the difficulty of getting general agreement on such matters as construction and manning standards. This was a familiar problem in IMCO, where a few maritime nations could always be depended upon to veto such efforts, if they seemed likely to result in a significant raising of the costs of commercial operation. It was hoped that the United States would take a responsible position on this, in the context of operational requirements for transit through the Northwest Passage, and that Canada in turn would recognize the distinction that can reasonably be drawn between standards for existing vessels and standards for vessels under construction.

So far the cabotage question has remained unresolved: it has not yet been declared whether Canada will treat all or part of the waters of the Canadian Arctic Archipelago as "coastal waters", within which only Canadian registered vessels would be permitted to operate. The alternative would be a quota arrangement, whereby a designated percentage of tonnage passing through would have to be under Canadian registration.

THE USE OF SHIP SIMULATION TECHNIQUES IN ARCTIC NAVIGATION

Dr. Ian R. McCallum*

I. INTRODUCTION

The economic pressures and energy requirements of the North American continent have caused a significant increase in extractive and transport activities in the Arctic regions of Alaska and Canada. The enormous reserves of oil and gas and other minerals in a politically stable, but physically difficult, geographic area have boosted technological innovation in a number of sectors. One of the most noticeable of these is the increased shipping activity in areas which were, until recently, not considered navigable for long periods of the year.

The oil- and gas-related shipping traffic is likely to be characterized by the exceptional size, cost, and complexity of the ships, by the hazardous nature and high value of their cargoes, by the very high economic and ecological consequences of accidents, and by the remoteness and severity of the environment. Thus, although the economic and political rewards resulting from this increased industrial and maritime activity may be enormous, it is clear that every step must be taken by industrial companies and regulatory bodies to ensure that these maritime operations are conducted under the safest conditions possible. There is always a potential conflict between commercial expediency and safety requirements, and this conflict is magnified by the peculiar operating conditions prevalent in the Arctic.

II. SHIP SAFETY: A RECURRING PROBLEM

The past decade has been one of intense innovation in ship design, and in the provision of new navigational aids and improved training requirements, and yet the annual casualty tonnage remains distressingly high. A few spectacular disasters, such as the stranding of the Amoco Cadiz, have focused attention on the possible scale of damage associated with oil-related cargoes, but still the casualty figures remain constant.

* Manager, Cardiff Ship Simulator, University of Wales Institute of Science & Technology. Cardiff, U.K.

What has become clear is that ship accidents are predominantly human-related, and such factors as the failure to keep a good lookout, poor passage planning, and inadequate bridge procedures are repeatedly identified as primary causes of casualties. Moreover, when new areas are opened up to shipping, or new types of ships are introduced to established routes, there is often no fund of knowledge of operating conditions and procedures on which to draw. There is thus no opportunity for pilots or ships' officers to learn safe and efficient procedures, except during actual maneuvers, with hazardous cargoes on board.

A particular lesson learned from the Amoco Cadiz disaster is the need for ships' officers to be aware of the behavior of their ship in a damaged condition. (Had the full effects of the use of stern-power been appreciated in the case of the Amoco Cadiz, it is possible that the grounding could have been avoided).

III. SHIP SIMULATION: A TOOL FOR RESEARCH AND TRAINING

As it becomes necessary to operate ships with hazardous cargoes in hostile and sensitive environments, the operational safety margins available are reduced, and conventional training methods become less applicable. It is not really feasible to teach ship-handling techniques for a new port area in the classroom, and ship owners are rarely willing to permit their ships to be used for evaluating maneuvering strategies at or near the limits of ship safety.

In the past few years, however, ship simulators have emerged as vital tools for both the design and evaluation of new port areas and for training ships' officers, pilots and port officers. The advantages of using simulation techniques in this way are now well known, but may be summarized as follows:

1. Conditions in the simulator are controllable and repeatable, so that operations may be carried out in precisely known conditions, and repeated as often as required. The behavior of trainees or research subjects may be observed and monitored.

2. Operations at or beyond the limits of ship safety may be carried out with no risk to ship or personnel, so that a range of alternative strategies may be evaluated and practiced.

3. A port area may be simulated long before it is actually built, and so operations peculiar to a particular port or sea area may be studied, and

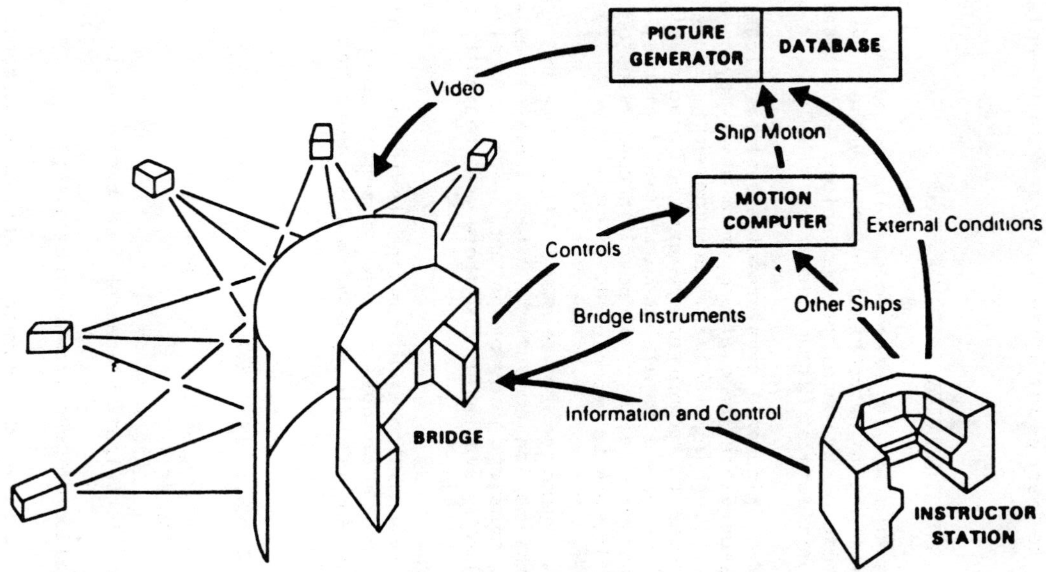

Figure 1. Cardiff Ship Simulator

operating personnel may become familiar with a new port before operations are actually started.

4. Operations in a simulator are cheaper, safer, and quicker to carry out than they are in a real environment.

IV. THE CARDIFF SHIP SIMULATOR (CASSIM)

A new, technologically advanced simulator is now being installed at Cardiff, to be operated jointly by the University of Wales Institute of Science and Technology (UWIST) and the South Glamorgan Institute of Higher Education (SGIHE) [1].

The Simulator (Figure 1) consists of a central bridge area mounted on a large vibration platform, from which may be seen, in color, the surrounding maritime environment. The visual scene is produced by computer-generated imagery (CGI) techniques, and can incorporate sea and land features, other ships and navigational aids. All possible conditions of daylight and visibility can be reproduced.

The ship's response to commands from the bridge is determined in the motion computer, and such effects as wind, waves, current, tugs and ice forces can be incorporated. A range of ship types is available, and these are constantly being added to.

Operations are controlled from the Instructor Station, which can introduce changes to environmental conditions, introduce other ships into the visual scene, and cause breakdowns to occur.

V. SIMULATION FOR ARCTIC NAVIGATION

The areas in which simulation techniques are most useful for Arctic operations are:

1. The design of navigation channels and port areas;

2. The evaluation of operational strategies;

3. Training operational personnel in bridge procedures and ship-handling techniques in normal and emergency conditions in ice;

4. Legal and regulatory topics, including the design of separation zones, the framing and evaluation of rules for safe navigation, the certification of ships' officers, pilots and port officers, and the analysis of accidents; and

5. Traffic growth analysis in channel design and provision of navigational aids, and degree of shore control.

For simulated Arctic operations, the simulator must be adapted in two ways: The visual scene must include the ice formations likely to be encountered, and the mathematical model of the ship must include the effects of the ice upon the ship. CASSIM is currently being modified in both these areas. The visual scene is able to incorporate both brash ice and icebergs of any size. The general effect of large ships in brash ice is now reasonably well known [2]. Ships tend to be more directionally stable and to have a larger turning circle, an effect not unlike that of operating in very shallow water. To this general effect must be added the resistive and impact forces of larger bodies of ice.

A. Design of Arctic Port Areas

Because of the immense support costs of Arctic operations, it is essential that designs for approach channels, jetties and navigation aid systems should be proven as far as possible before construction is started. The use of a simulator enables dynamic design criteria to be used, by considering the ship, operator, and environment as a dynamic system, as opposed to static rules of thumb [3]. Matters such as the optimum alignment of a jetty, the width and radius of curvature of approach channels, and the size of a turning basin can all be designed with greater confidence if alternative designs are tried out in simulation before building. The savings in cost of unnecessary dredging can more than pay for the whole simulator study.

There are at present few firm guidelines on the design of navigation aid systems, and recent simulator-based studies have shown that substantially better navigation can be obtained by using optimum buoyage layouts and sector light design. The cost of altering an unsatisfactory design after installation is very high, particularly in Arctic areas.

B. Operational Strategies

An integral part of a port's overall design is the pattern of ship operations associated with it. There will in general be a range of operational strategies which are feasible and which will get a ship in without damage. Some will, however, have a far higher safety margin than others, and it is desirable to evaluate the whole range of feasible options to determine the optimum operational behavior. Operational strategies will vary significantly with weather conditions, and the number and power of tugs available, and so the simulator can ideally be used to establish a "safe environmental envelope" within which operations can be undertaken with minimum risk.

It is important also to develop and evaluate a range of strategies to cope with the effects of failure of ship equipment, and consideration can be given to incorporating escape zones into the port design to minimize the effects of such failures.

C. Training and Familiarization

Once optimum strategies have been developed, ship and port operators can be trained in their use, both under normal conditions of operation and also under extreme weather conditions and with ship failures. The ability to simulate critical or near-critical conditions is seen as being particularly valuable, as most ship operators rarely experience the difficulties of operating near the limits of safety at any time during their career. The ability to simulate a port area before it is built enables all those responsible for navigation (ships' officers, pilots and marine officers) to become familiar with the port's design and with the pattern of operations before the first ship comes in. Training in bridge procedures and teamwork can also be given to ensure a uniformly high standard of performance.

D. Legal and Regulatory Topics

The simulator's potential as a tool for research into the problems of shipping control has only very recently become fully appreciated. As new sea areas are developed, some form of traffic control using separation zones frequently becomes necessary and this may be combined with varying degrees of shore control by marine officers. Under hazardous environmental conditions, control may become mandatory rather than purely advisory. Because of the ability of the simulator to work with a very large data base, it is possible to simulate the whole of a proposed separation zone, and evaluate its effectiveness under various operating conditions with differing degrees of shore control. This can of course be done long before the details of the separation zone or the shipping control rules are finalized.

In the aircraft industry, the use of simulators for certification of pilots is universally accepted. The maritime community, however, has been most reluctant to accept that simulators can be used to assist in the granting of operators' licenses in this way. A notable exception has been the Port of Valdez, where a certain proportion of the qualifying time for masters requiring certification for the port can be obtained in a simulator. This use of the simulator is considered to be most useful when operations into a new port area are under consideration and there is no significant operating experience to draw upon.

Radar simulators have for some years been used to analyze accidents [4], and it is considered that much valuable information can be obtained by re-creating the circumstances of the accident in simulation. In particular, it should be possible in many cases to determine which series of events was not possible for physical reasons. Again, in the situation, the dynamic properties of the simulator are available as an investigative tool.

VI. CONCLUSION

The exploitation of the Arctic region is one of the greatest technological challenges to mankind, and the consequences of error are dramatic in both economic and ecological terms. The ship simulator enables a whole range of new techniques to be brought to bear which will ensure that the risks of maritime disaster are known and can be minimized. No major maritime development should proceed without these techniques being used to the fullest.

NOTES

1. McCallum, I.R. and Rawson, A.J., "The Cardiff Ship Simulator-Design Features and Operational Philosophy," (Paper presented at the Second International Conference on Marine Simulation held at New York on June 1-5,1981), pp. E1-1 to E1-11.

2. Eda, H., "Maneuvering Characteristics of Great Lake Ships," (Proceedings of the Fourth CAORF Symposium held on September 29-30, 1980 at the National Maritime Research Center, New York).

3. McCallum, I.R., "Marine Simulators in Port Design," (Dock and Harbour Authority, August 1978).

4. Burger, W. and Corbet, A.G., "Court Cases and Radar," Nautical Review, Vol. 1 No. 9 (November 1978), pp. 40-42.

THE LAW OF THE SEA INSTITUTE

LIST OF PARTICIPANTS

Vera Alexander
Institute of Marine Sciences
University of Alaska

Scott Allen
Law of the Sea Institute
University of Hawaii

Gordon Beanlands
Inst. for Resource & Environ.
Studies, Dalhousie University

Richard Bilder
Faculty of Law
University of Wisconsin

Lincoln Bloomfield
Dept. of Political Science
Mass. Institute of Technology

Francois Bregha
Arctic Seas Program (CARC)
Canadian Arctic Resource Cte.

William E. Butler
Faculty of Law
University Colege London

Jack Davidson
Sea Grant
University of Hawaii

Max Dunbar
Marine Science Centre
McGill University

Robert L. Friedheim
Inst. for Marine & Coastal Studies
Univ. of Southern California

Paul Fye
Woods Hole Oceanographic
Institution

Frank Griffiths
Dept. of Political Economy
University of Toronto

Donn Haglund
Dept. of Geography
Univ. of Wisconsin

Howard Hume
Envir. Protection Group
Petro-Canada Exploration

Douglas M. Johnston
Dalhousie Ocean Studies
Program

Lyn E. Lewis
Inst. of Ocean Science
Sidney, British Columbia

Ian McCallum
Dept. of Maritime Studies
Univ. of Wales Institute

Michael MccGwire
Brookings Institution
Washington, D.C.

Suzanne McQuinn
Dalhousie Ocean Studies
Program

Edward Miles
Inst. of Marine Studies
Univ. of Washington

Hal Mills
Mills Consulting Services
Halifax, Nova Scotia

Donald Munton
Dept. of Political Science
Dalhousie University

Ned Ostenso
National Oceanic &
Atmospheric Administration
Washington, D.C.

Donat Pharand
Faculty of Law
University of Ottawa

Ruth I. Thompson
Dalhousie Ocean Studies
Programme

William Westermeyer
Dept. of Political Science
Univ. of Southern California

A. Wiggins
Legal Division
Imperial Oil Company

William Winsor
Centre for Cold Resources
Memorial University